Fated to Defeat

33rd Waffen-Grenadier Division der SS 'Charlemagne' in the Struggle for Pomerania 1945

Łukasz Gładysiak

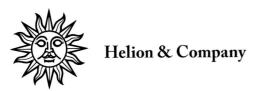

Helion & Company

Helion & Company Limited
Unit 8 Amherst Business Centre
Budbrooke Road
Warwick
CV34 5WE
England
Tel. 01926 499 619
Email: info@helion.co.uk
Website: www.helion.co.uk
Twitter: @helionbooks
Visit our blog at blog.helion.co.uk

Published by Helion & Company 2021
Designed and typeset by Mary Woolley (www.battlefield-design.co.uk)
Cover designed by Paul Hewitt, Battlefield Design (www.battlefield-design.co.uk)

Text and translation © Łukasz Gładysiak 2020
Images © as individually credited

ISBN 978-1-912866-17-5

British Library Cataloguing-in-Publication Data.
A catalogue record for this book is available from the British Library.

For details of other military history titles published by Helion & Company Limited contact the above address, or visit our website: http://www.helion.co.uk.

We always welcome receiving book proposals from prospective authors.

Contents

List of Illustrations

Introduction

On 20 January 1945, in the German 2nd Military District Headquarters in Szczecin (Stettin), the Gneisenau Alarm was announced. The alert – which on the one hand was to launch a number of actions aimed at evacuating the administration and civilians of the region stretched along the eastern part of the southern shore of the Baltic Sea, and on the other to mobilize all forces and means to oppose the enemy attacking from at least two directions – clearly confirmed that the Second World War had eventually reached the borders of *Provinz* Pommern (Pomerania). Its inhabitants, especially those who were German, were to discover the brutal consequences of this situation in the coming weeks. The conflict unleashed by the Germans nearly six years earlier was already tilted in favour of the anti-Nazi coalition.

There were members of foreign branches of the *Waffen-SS* among the military units still faithful to Adolf Hitler who were to defend the borders and residents of the province, including a group of several thousand citizens of the French Republic that had been conquered in 1940 by the Third Reich. They were part of a group of nearly 20,000 French inhabitants who, during the Second World War, openly supported the Berlin regime. They pulled together under the banner of their recent enemy for various reasons, ranging from typically ideological ones to the desire to hide from revengeful countrymen. What is certain, however, is that when the first echelon with members of the *33. Waffen-Grenadier Division der SS 'Charlemagne'* rolled into the railway station in what is now Czarne in Poland (Hammerstein in 1945), where the group commanded by *SS-Brigadeführer* Gustav Krukenberg began its Pomeranian epic, hardly anyone still believed in a favourable conclusion to the conflict for Germany.

This volume attempts to systematise the state of research into and chronological order of activities of the *'Charlemagne'* Division during the fighting for Pomerania, which lasted from the end of February to the second half of March 1945. The author has great hopes that this work will provide an impulse for further exploring this history. For the English reader, it is an attempt to describe the last weeks of the Second World War in Pomerania as the conflict spread across Poland.

As part of the volume introduction, the situation for the French after the successful German military operation known as Plan Yellow (*Fall Gelb*) and the occupation of France from June 1940 are briefly presented. In addition, attention is paid to the events that a few months before the fall of Adolf Hitler led to the formation of an independent division composed of citizens of the Third French Republic. The most important of these events are included, namely the battles of the Legion of French Volunteers against Bolshevism (LVF) and the actions of the *Waffen-Grenadier Brigade der SS 'Charlemagne'* in 1944. The whole is supplemented with tables and biographies of selected soldiers, which can be found in the appendix. It is worth noting that in order to make it easier for the reader to navigate both the modern and pre-war topography of *Provinz* Pommern, the names of Pomeranian towns appearing in the text are each time given in two forms: current (Polish) and that valid until late spring 1945 (German). They are also collected in the form of a separate appendix.

Analysing the military operations of the *33. Waffen-Grenadier Division der SS 'Charlemagne'* in Pomerania, one should pay attention to the various catalogue of sources. The author has used nearly seventy of these; their collection and elaboration took over seven years. Among them you can find documents published by the staff of Army Group Vistula – the formation superior to all large units in *Provinz* Pommern in the late period of the Third Reich – preserved primarily in the United States National Archives. They are supplemented with wartime maps. Interesting, especially from the point of view of individual stories, are accounts and memoirs, both officially published and obtained privately by the author. Among these, and deserving critical attention, are Christian La Mazière's notes, published in 2005, which are the first and so far the only book published in Polish on the subject of the French SS volunteers in the struggle for Pomerania. Detailed knowledge of the history of the unit is also possible thanks to the unpublished memories of two other soldiers: Alain Boutier and Robert Soulat. Superior analysis, carried out in the 1950s, is contained in a book (published in 2010) by Felix Steiner, commander of the *III. SS-Panzerkorps*, and later the *11. SS-Panzer-Armee*. There were also volunteer threads in the memoirs of soldiers of the Polish Army in the East, primarily in the notes of Alojzy Sroga, who in the 1970s managed to gather an extensive account of the siege of Kołobrzeg (Kolberg) in March 1945. In this case, there is no shortage of references to confrontation with the French soldiers of the *Waffen-SS*.

In the historical literature of a scientific and popular-scientific nature, particular attention should be paid to the work of Helmut Lindenblatt, who in 2008 published a fundamental book on the fighting in Pomerania entitled *Pommern 1945. Eines der letzten Kapitel in der Geschichte vom Untergant des Dritten Reiches*. In the context of volunteers in the German Army as a whole, nothing can beat the four-volume study by David Littlejohn, *Foreign Legions of the Third Reich*, published in the United States in the 1980s. For the subject of this publication, analyses by Robert Forbes, Richard Landwehr, Eric Lefèvre and Jean Mabire are extremely valuable.

This publication could not have been created without the commitment and help of many people, who for many years undertook in their professional life – or as a hobby – research into the subject of the late Second World War in Western Pomerania, and agreed that I could use the results of their work.

The author would like to especially thank Robert Soulat (who died in 2015), who, despite the often-difficult situation in which the participants of the volunteer *Waffen-SS* units were in their native countries, overcame obstacles to use their memoirs, which allowed the telling of episodes that have not been widely known until now. He would like also to thank Mikołaj Jagora for sharing his knowledge in a correspondence that lasted several years; Vincent Domergue, the first critical reader of the typescript of this book; and Stanisław Kłoskowski from Olszanów (Elsenau in 1945), without whose information and help it would be almost impossible to reconstruct events taking place in the vicinity of the city of Czarne. Another man who helped with the subject is both the director of the Museum of Greater Poland Insurgents in Luboń and the author's cordial colleague, Michał Krzyżaniak, who shared a wide collection of archives related to the Army Group Vistula.

The author owes individual expressions of gratitude to the members of the Polish Historical Re-enactment Association '*Die Freiwilligen*', which from the beginning of its activities has focused on exploring knowledge about the activities of the French in the Pomeranian campaign, in particular: Łukasz Dyczkowski, Maciej Wilczyński and Tomasz Zdanowicz, as well as one of the precursors of research on foreign *Waffen-SS* units in Poland, Tomasz Borowski. He also recognizes the help of Grzegorz Kruk, thanks to whom, in 2011, he had the opportunity to participate in field research related to the history of the '*Charlemagne*' Division conducted in the vicinity of Białogard (Belgard an der Persante) and Karlino (Körlin), and Maciej Cichecki, for the opportunity to illustrate the content with original artifacts related to the formation.

The accompanying images would not have been possible without the involvement of director Aleksander Ostasz and employees of the Museum of Polish Arms in Kołobrzeg, thanks to whom the author had the opportunity to conduct a wide photographic query. This resulted in a set of little-known photographs taken in February and March 1945 in Pomerania. The museum has also kindly agreed to be the official patron of this publication.

Finally, the author would like to thank his wife, Weronica, thanks to whom, after changing their place of residence from Wielkopolska to the Western Pomeranian Voivodeship, he became interested in the history of this region. Throughout the creation of this publication, she has been patient and understanding with the author's many dilemmas, fully supporting him on each occasion.

Białogard (Belgard an der Persante), November 2020

1

Collapse of the Third French Republic

Some 125,000 recruits from the occupied countries or outside the Third Reich participated in military operations on the side of Germany during the Second World War.[1] Each of them, most often according to the idea of the so-called 'anti-Bolshevik Crusade', which the Berlin authorities formally announced in the summer of 1941 – but which had been the subject of propaganda for much longer – decided to spill blood side by side with members of the *Wehrmacht*. Among them were citizens of the Third French Republic, which had been defeated in June 1940. It was these Frenchmen who participated first in bloody battles in the northern sector of the Eastern Front, and then, under the aegis of the *Schutzstaffeln* (*SS*), in today's Poland. For many, the war – which the Nazi regime was unable to win, even for purely material reasons – ended in 1944 in the territory of Galicia or, a few months later, in areas that are now part of the Western Pomeranian Voivodeship in Poland. Before moving on to the historical analysis of the *33. Waffen-Grenadier Division der SS 'Charlemagne'*, we should look at the genesis of the phenomenon of French recruitment in the ranks of the German armed forces. It is worth mentioning that throughout its history, France has very often appeared as the natural opponent of Germany, often because of the disputed neighbourhood of the Rhineland.

Diplomatic successes achieved in the second half of the 1930s by Berlin were followed by a series of almost bloodless conflicts, which historians today call the *Blumenkriege* (Flowers Wars). These included incorporating Austria (the *Anschluss*), the Sudetenland and the port of Klaipeda in Lithuania, as well as, shortly before the beginning of the second global conflict, the partition of Czechoslovakia and creation of the completely subordinate Slovakian state. These events meant that in many European countries at the time, including the Great War victors France and Great Britain, National Socialism appeared not only as a military power, but also an economic hegemon, which despite international restrictions was able to come out of the Great Depression almost exclusively by its own efforts. This feeling was confirmed by the allied states in

---

1   G. Williamson, *The SS: Hitler's Instrument of Terror* (London: 1995), p. 109.

the West not reacting militarily to the conquest of Poland in September and October 1939, which was followed by the collapse of Denmark, Norway, Belgium and the Netherlands in the face of German aggression. This culminated in the defeat and humiliation of the Third French Republic, confirmed by the parade of the German *87. Infanterie-Division* in the Champs Elysees in Paris on 14 June 1940.

Regardless of military victories, for many of the young generation of Europeans, the national-socialist order appeared as a new and in many respects attractive model of the state. "People saw in Hitler a kind of 'messiah' who solved the problem of unemployment, outlawed communism in Germany and freed the country from the shackles of the Versailles Pact," wrote one of the volunteers in the *SS-Standarte Westland*, Dutchman Hendrik Verton, many decades after the end of the Second World War.[2] This is confirmed by the words of Léon Degrelle, the leader of the Belgian Rexist movement and one of the leading proponents of the idea of cooperation between the Western European community and the Third Reich, which were delivered during a meeting of supporters of national socialism in Madrid in the 1980s:

> Hitler was a people's tribune, a man who managed to solve the problem of unemployment in an unprecedented dimension to this day. Over two years, he created jobs for six million Germans, getting rid of the problem of increasing poverty. In five years, the income of the average German worker doubled without inflation. Hundreds of thousands of homes were built that workers could buy at a minimal price. Each of these houses had a garden. All factory complexes had been enriched with sports facilities and swimming pools. Paid holidays for workers were introduced for the first time.[3]

Although from today's perspective it is not difficult to understand that all these activities were largely aimed at mobilizing German society for the planned conquest of Europe, from the point of view of the second half of the 1930s, or even the beginning of the following decade, this type of rhetoric found its way onto fertile ground. In addition, the German state, led by Adolf Hitler – pushing ideological issues aside – appeared to be a perfectly organized creation, where assessment was not evaluated by class origin, but by merit and skill, so everyone could climb high up the career ladder. In this context, the criminal activities busily concealed by Berlin, even in occupied Poland, and violations of international conventions in France itself – exemplified by the shooting at Le Paradis of almost 100 British prisoners of war by soldiers of the *SS-Totenkopf-Division* on 27 May 1940 – seemed imperceptible.

2   H. Verton, *W piekle frontu wschodniego. Byłem holenderskim ochotnikiem w Waffen-SS* (Warsaw: 2010), p. 35.
3   L. Degrelle, 'The History of the *Waffen-SS*', speech at the forum of the Asociación Cultural 'Amigos de Léon Degrelle'.

Regardless of the feelings of the French, or residents of other Western European countries, at least from 1938, Berlin promoted the slogan of unifying Europe under common banners. Many of the nearly 9-million-strong representatives of groups such as Scandinavians, Flemish (also, from 1943, residents of the Catholic part of Belgium, the Walloons), Dutch and even English were said to be predestined to participate in the implementation of the policy of *Herrenvolk*, i.e., a continent arranged according to a new national-socialist pattern. This course of action had its genesis in contemporary German anthropology, whose 'achievements' were legitimized by many of the world's leading researchers. At the top of the hierarchy the Nazis chose was the Nordic race. It belonged to her primarily from birth, though, which was emphasized in her memories by the commander of the German *III. SS-Panzerkorps*, also known as the '*Germanisches*' ('Germanic'), *SS-Obergruppenführer* Felix Steiner, in the initial period of recruitment of those who did not have German citizenship, which was crucial for joining the German armed forces, but also the society of the Third Reich, there was an appropriate ideological attitude and faith in the right direction set out by decision-makers in Berlin.

These slogans found fertile ground. As early as 1938, 20 foreigners joined the *Wehrmacht* banners even before war was declared. Two years later, there were already 100 of them, including 44 neutral Swiss citizens, three Swedes and five Americans.[4] In December 1939, the *Ergänzungsamt der Waffen-SS* – Waffen-SS Recruitment Office – was created in the capital of the Third Reich. Although the task of this institution, supervised by the then *SS-Standartenführer* Gottlob Berger (later head of the SS-Main Office), was primarily to involve ethnic Germans from the occupied countries, mainly the former Czechoslovakia, in the armed arm of the *Schutzstaffel* (*SS*), it was also charged with registration of potential volunteers of other nationalities. This was to meet the demand of the German Army's corps during the first spring of the war. For example, in the ranks of the *SS-Totenkopf-Division*, out of about 20,000 soldiers, some 13,000 exceeded the age limit for conscription, coming from the ranks of police formations or units serving in the concentration camps. This meant that, in the opinion of military experts, they were, in the words of the author of a well-known book published in Britain, Edmund Blandford, low-value combat material.[5] On the other hand, the need to reach for recruits from abroad was caused by the difficult relationship between the *Waffen-SS* and the regular German Army. Despite the fact that the growth of the *Waffen-SS*, whose number exceeded 100,000 in the summer of 1940, met with a cold and often reluctant reaction from the generals, Germany's land forces – as well as its *Luftwaffe* and *Kriegsmarine* – needed strengthening. Their attention was primarily directed at the indigenous citizens of the Third Reich, the so-called *Reichsdeutsche*. In the end, however, it was decided to compromise, which resulted in delegating approximately two-thirds of the recruitment to the ranks of the

4   F. Steiner, *Ochotnicy Waffen-SS. Idea i poświęcenie* (Gdańsk: 2010), p. 32.
5   E. Blandford, *Hitler's Second Army ...* , p. 83.

land forces, and the rest to the aviation and navy. From this first group, recruits for the *Waffen-SS* were to be regularly separated based on the needs reported on an ongoing basis. This system initially proved to be inefficient. According to forecasts made in the second half of 1940, the army could deploy at most 12,000 young Germans to fill the approximately 18,000 vacancies needed to fill the *Schutzstaffel* units. It is also worth noting that since June 1940, the search for reinforcements began outside the borders of Germany. On 23 June, a subversive military group codenamed *Erna* was formed, supervised by German military intelligence (*Abwehr*) made up of Estonians who emigrated to Germany after being captured by the Red Army.[6] In April of the following year, the first full-scale training camp for residents of the Baltic states was established on the Hanko Peninsula in Finland.

The idea of the so-called anti-Bolshevik crusade was important for enlistment in virtually all of Europe. There is no doubt that after the experience of the first two years of the Weimar Republic – including the almost full-scale civil war in 1918–19, in which representatives of the extreme left wing stood on one side of the front line, with on the other, members of the army and units faithful to the new authorities, such as the *Freikorps* – German society for the most part looked with great fear at the Union of Soviet Socialist Republics, the matrix of communism. Moreover, the leading representatives of the state of Lenin and Stalin, as well as the main executors of their orders, were associated with Jews. According to leading ideologists of the Third Reich, the destructive force of such a marriage was regularly seen, from Biblical times, through the devastation Europe suffered in the first half of the 17th century, the Seven Years' War and the French Revolution, up to the overthrow of Tsarist Russia.[7] The infamous book *Myth of the 20th century*, Alfred Rosenberg's basic interpretation of contemporary politics in Germany, swarned that by the middle of the seventh decade of the 20th century, Bolshevism would become a fully fledged militant religion, which, like Islam before it, would threaten the existence of European civilization. It was emphasized by Rosenberg that the new war, which inevitably was to take place in the eastern part of the continent, would not only be an armed clash between two states (in this case, the Third Reich and the USSR), but an ideological class conflict outside the framework of international law, and hence governed by its own laws.[8] It was stressed that the final victory would require the trans-national effort of all who valued the achievements of European civilization to date. This war was also to be preventive in nature.[9]

There was an intensification of anti-Bolshevik propaganda when the Third Reich conquered its neighbours in the West. This was initially addressed primarily to Danes,

6   C. Jurado, *Germany's Eastern Front Allies (2). Baltic Forces* (Oxford: 2002), p. 5.
7   H. Himmler, *Die Schutzstaffeln als antibolschewistische Kampforganisation* (Munich: 1937), pp. 3-6.
8   T. Ripley, *Hitler's Praetorians*, p. 53.
9   It is worthy of mention that, according to *Mein Kampf*, the German–Soviet war would begin the liberation of the Russian states. M. Szopa, *Przestrzeń dla rasy panów*, [w:] 'II wojna światowa. Wydarzenia – ludzie – bojowe szlaki', part IV, pp. 10–11.

Flemish, Dutch and Norwegians. Already, on 9 June 1940, before the surrender of France, recruitment began into the ranks of the *SS-Standarte Westland* – the first, Dutch branch of the *Waffen-SS* – headed by *SS-Standartenführer* Hilmar Wäckerle, the first commander of the concentration camp in Dachau. At the same time, there was also enlisting by the *SS* of Scandinavians, who were included in *SS-Standartenführer* Fritz von Scholz's *SS-Standarte Nordland*. Both groupings later joined the first international unit operating as a corps, the *5. SS-Division 'Wiking'*. It is also worth mentioning that in the summer of 1940, British citizens were also called upon to form units to join the fight against Bolshevism, the Nazis even proposing the exchange of British prisoners of war in the Dunkirk area for men of working age who were willing to work for and serve the Third Reich.[10]

Shortly thereafter, the Berlin-controlled press throughout occupied Europe was flooded with information confirming the criminal nature of Stalin's dictatorship. Extensive material condemned the profaning of places of worship by the Soviet authorities, with 'crimes' described in the finest detail, indicating that existence in a 'Communist Paradise' inevitably led to destruction or slave labour. There were also posters on the walls of the major cities of the continent encouraging recruitment into German ranks, referring to the brotherhood of arms, power or historical episodes important for individual nations, such as, for example, Viking expeditions, which were used in national-socialist rhetoric in Norway and Denmark. They were accompanied by frequent appearances of leading Nazi figures, such as *Reichsführer-SS* Heinrich Himmler, who repeatedly said: "We must unite for ourselves all who have Nordic blood, which will knock out weapons from our opponent and ensure that never again will German blood be shed against us."[11]

Léon Degrelle reminded us many years after the end of the war that such words were not without response:

> Our hands were immaculate, our hearts were clean, our love of our homeland was bright and flaming, free from any compromises ... In 1941, unexpectedly, we were given the opportunity to become the companions of the winners' weapons, completely equal to them. The admiration expressed by young Europeans towards the SS was by all means a natural phenomenon ... It was not Europe but the sense of community of the German race that pushed them towards conscription. They identified with the victorious Germany. Hitler was the person they [had] waited for [for] a long time ... Before his appearance, German imperialism was associated only with the exploitation of the occupied countries, without offering anything in return. Suddenly, a man offering a great idea appeared in place of the looting: social equality that had been pulsing through their veins for years. [There was a] broadly understood New Order

10   E. Blandford, *Hitler's Second Army*, pp. 84–85.
11   G. Williamson, *The SS: Hitler's ...*, p. 108.

in place of pre-war cosmopolitanism, characteristic of supposed 'democratic states'.[12]

Similarly, many foreign private soldiers were strongly influenced by the initially carefully selected recruitment from among distinguished *Waffen-SS* officers of staff to train foreign recruits. Hendrik Werton, who was serving in the ranks of the *SS-Standarte Westland*, wrote: "Personal contacts with German soldiers, their proper behaviour in occupied countries, which was impressive, played an important role. Perfect military machinery not only shocked, but also fascinated many young and adult people in the area occupied by Germany. Many also believed that after the final victory of the Third Reich, almost everyone who took an active part in the crusade against the USSR would receive an appropriate reward in return." This was the vision of, among others, the leader of the Belgian Rexists: if National Socialist Germany were victorious, then they would become the master of the wonderfully fertile land in the East, connected to them by rail networks, rivers and canals, open to the German genius of organization and production. The rebirth of the great German Reich, based on a perfect social foundation, stretching from the North Sea to the Black Sea and the Volga, would be such a power, would be so attractive, offering 20 nations crammed in the Old Continent so much development that its territories would undoubtedly become the starting point for the creation of the European federation that Napoleon had wanted.[13]

A further argument in favour of joining the armed effort of the Third Reich was the desire to improve a recruit's property status or escape from the reality of occupation. Like in the *Schutzstaffel* study, author Gordon Williamson has stated that young Scandinavians collaborating with the forces of occupation, or those from Belgium, the Netherlands or France, saw the possibility of avoiding forced labour or gaining access to better food that was issued only in German canteens, and even, in the case of loyal service, full German citizenship. It also seemed attractive to join the ranks of a well-organized, almost monastic community or a prosaic search for adventure. Later, with the spectre of invasion by the anti-Hitler coalition forces in Europe clearly on the horizon, enlistment into the ranks of the *Wehrmacht* or *Waffen-SS* and departure in units to the front could become a method of avoiding responsibility for earlier pro-German actions after the liberation of their homeland by the Allies. In the case of the French, the revenge of their countrymen would primarily be against members of the militia of Vichy France, the *Milice Française*, or those actively engaged in the fight against the underground Resistance and the extermination of the Jewish militia, the French Guards (*Les Gardes Françaises*). One such example was a soldier of the *33. Waffen-Grenadier Division der SS 'Charlemagne'*, Christian La Maziere, who joined

---

12   L. Degrelle, *Front wschodni 1941–1945* (Kraków: 2007), pp. 8–9.
13   Ibid., p. 15.

the then *Waffen-Grenadier Brigade der SS 'Charlemagne'* in August 1944, thanks to which he was able to leave France with the retreating *Wehrmacht* units.[14]

Whereas in the Scandinavian countries and the Netherlands in the late 1930s, the authorities in Berlin tried to push pro-German sentiment, their efforts in France – which was, as already stated, a natural opponent of the Third Reich – were rather marginal until the conquest of that country. The leading political groups supporting cooperation between France and Hitler were formed in 1938 and had their own paramilitary model: the *Allgemeine-SS* – the so-called Black Guard (*Garde Noir*) – the French National Socialist Party (*Parti Français National-Socialiste*), under the leadership of Christien Massage, and the French Crusade for National Socialism (*La Croisade Française du National-Socialisme*), led by Maurice-Bernard de la Gatinais.[15] Their position changed after the *Wehrmacht*'s successful implementation of *Fall Gelb*, with a rapid breakthrough on the western border of France and overwhelming victory. Despite France having emerged as an apparent superpower from the signing of the Treaty of Versailles 20 years previously, after just over a month of military operations, on 15 June 1940, the French government fled from Paris to Bordeaux, and two days later, President Albert Lebrun appointed Marshal Philippe Pétain, the hero of Verdun, as prime minister. On the same day, he announced his readiness for France to lay down their arms at the invaders' feet. On 22 June, at 1850 hours local time, in the railroad car in Compiegne that was symbolic for both nations as the location for the completion of the armistice ending the Great War, German General Wilhelm Keitel and a representative of the Third Republic, General Charles Huntziger, signed the ceasefire which in practice meant France's unconditional surrender. On 10 July, the French National Assembly gathered in Toulouse and, against the will of the president, gave extraordinary powers to Marshal Pétain, who on this basis proclaimed himself *L'Etat Français*, the Head of the French State. His deputy and head of government was Pierre Laval, who was in favour of cooperation with Germany. A new stage had begun in the history of the French state, with what is known today as Vichy France. This was a quasi-autonomous state covering about a third of the pre-war area of the country. The rest, including the capital, was under occupation. This situation was to have positive effects for supporters of national socialism in France.

On 25 July 1940, the formation began – with the full cooperation of the Third Reich – of the French Guard (*Gardes Françaises*), which was announced in the pages of the Paris-based nationalist and anti-Semitic magazine *Au Pilori* (*Under the Pillory*) by the initiator of the formation, lawyer Robert Petit. In a short time, recruitment modelled on German lines was introduced into its ranks, whose members, in addition to having the necessary ideological attitude, had to be 18 years old. The group's headquarters was in a house that had previously belonged to the Jewish Rosenthal family at 28

14   Ch. de La Mazière, *Marzyciel w hełmie. Francuz w Waffen SS* (Warsaw: 2005), pp. 13–19.
15   T. Szarota, *U progu zagłady. Zajścia antyżydowskie i pogromy w okupowanej Europie – Warszawa, Paryż, Amsterdam, Antwerpia, Kowno* (Warsaw: 2000), p. 139.

Champs-Élysées. Both the French Guard, commanded by Charles Lefebvre, and its youth wing the Young Front (*Jeune Front*, for those aged 14–18), under Robert Hersaut, became infamous for their assaults on shops run by Jews. The attacks mirrored those carried out by the Nazi Party's Brown Shirts (*Sturmabteilungen, SA*) in mid-1930s Germany.[16]

Vichy France also favoured the emergence of other radical groups from the shadows. One of them was the French People's Party (*Parti Populaire Française*), which paradoxically originated from the St Denis area of Paris in June 1934 with an extremely leftist core. At the head of this faction, which in 1940 could count on the support of up to a quarter of a million citizens,[17] was Jacques Doriot, a former communist and participant in the Spanish Civil War. Although the group was formally active only in areas managed by the Vichy government, its cells, most likely with the tacit consent of the German authorities, also functioned in the occupied part of France, where citizens were not formally allowed to associate with any political groups. The armed arm of the French People's Party was the Order Service (*Service d'Ordre*) for those aged 18–50, while its youth wing, the French People's Youth (*Jeunesse Populaire Française*), had the assault section *Groupe d'Action* and the *Corps Franc de la jeunesse*.[18] Jacques Doriot's group was extremely valuable for the Germans, since from the beginning its members were not only Jews but also communists. In addition, it was supported by nationalist-oriented French financiers, headed by Bank Worms director Gabriel Leroy-Ladurie. The *Parti Populaire Française* also provided financial support in the form of 300,000 francs to the fascist government of Italy.[19]

Members of the French Party (*Parti Franciste*), led by Marcel Bucard from September 1933, were in favour of transforming France into a fascist state organized according to its own pattern. It also had its own armed wing, the French Corps (*Corps Francs*), and from 1943 the French Legion (*Franciste Legion*) with an elite *Main Bleue* section. It is worth noting that the youth militia *Jeunesse Franciste* created as part of this faction was the only one functioning legally within the borders of the French state from 1942. When Germany invaded the Soviet Union in June 1941, the first French military group operating under the *Wehrmacht* was formed, the Legion of French Volunteers against Bolshevism (*Légion des volontaires français contre le bolchevisme*).

On 13 December 1940, in the part of the country run by Pétain's Vichy regime, the National People's Assembly (*Rassemblement National Populaire*) was formed, whose creator and chairman was Marcel Déat, a former associate of the socialist party and Minister of Aviation in the government of Albert Sarraut during the mid-1930s. Supported by around 21,000 compatriots, they advocated full submission to Berlin,

---

16 *Ibid.*, pp. 107–08.
17 O. Pigoreau, *Rendez-vous tragique à Mengen*, [w:] 'Batailles. Histoire Militaire du XXe Siècle', No. 34 (Paris: 2009), pp. 52–61.
18 D. Littlejohn, *Foreign Legions of the Third Reich. Vol. 1: Norway, Denmark, France* (San Jose: 1979), pp. 117–18.
19 O. Pigoreau, *Rendez-vous tragique…*, pp. 68–69.

promoting a policy of collaboration. At the same time, this faction was in opposition to the Vichy government, often accusing the Head of the French State of conspiring with Jews against Germany. Like other political groups, an armed militia was formed, the National People's Legion (*Légion Nationale Populaire*), transformed in 1943 into the National People's Milice (*Milice Nationale Populaire*), along with a youth group, the *Jeunesse Nationale Populaire*, under the command of Roland Silly.[20]

Perhaps the most radical, nationalist and pro-German views were represented by members of the Revolutionary Social Movement (*Mouvement Social Révolutionnaire*) led by Eugène Deloncle, who was once associated with the terrorist group *Kaptur* (*La Cagoule*), which in the autumn of 1937 was broken by the French police. In their case, great emphasis was put on close cooperation with Germany, as a result of which it was this faction, under the code name the Secret Committee of the Revolutionary Action (*Comité Secrète d'Action Revolutionnaire*), that become the main tool to deal with the French extreme left, and primarily the Jewish population (in this sphere, Deloncle's supporters worked closely with the *SS*-Security Service, the *Sicherheitsdienst*).[21]

Ideologically appropriate recruits were additionally provided by a number of smaller political groups that, remaining on the margins of the Third Republic scene, were given the chance to appear after its fall. These included, for example, the right-wing movement of Charles Maurras which originated in the late 19th century, French Action (Anti-British, Anti-Semitic and Anti-Bolshevik League) – *Ligue Française Anti-Brittanique, Anti-Sémitique et Anti-Bolchevique* – led by a French-born officer in the French Army, Pierre Constantini; the French Front (*Front Franc*), under Jean Boissel; the French National Collective Party (*Parti Français National-Collectiviste*) of Pierre Clémenti; the Party of Breton Nationalists (*Parti Nationaliste Breton*); and finally French Social Progress (*Progrès Social Français*). Support for the Vichy authorities and the German occupation was also demonstrated by a number of smaller youth organizations and some veterans. A similar attitude, after the *Wehrmacht* began its occupation of all French territory in November 1942, was manifested by members of the National Revolutionary Front (*Front Révolutionnaire National*), under the leadership of the former communist Henri Barbé.

---

20   D. Littlejohn, *Foreign Legions of...*, pp. 120–24.
21   Littlejohn, *Political Traitors* (London: 1972), p. 215.

2

From *Wehrmacht* Legion to SS Brigade

Although, according to initial assumptions, no more Frenchmen were expected to fight for Hitler's Germany – and even they, compared to, for example, citizens of the Scandinavian countries or the Netherlands, were in most cases distant from the brotherhood of arms with Germany – the authorities in Berlin decided to use the extensive French political scene to implement a propaganda campaign and then carry out a first wave of recruitment in France.

On 22 June 1941, the day the *Wehrmacht* launched Operation Barbarossa against the Soviet Union, the largest military operation in the history of warfare, the anti-Bolshevik crusade became a reality. Over 4.7 million men in 164 divisions under the banners of the Third Reich and a number of allied countries launched an attack along a front extending from the southern coast of the Baltic Sea to the Black Sea. The offensive took the Soviets completely by surprise, their defences having been weakened as a result of decisions taken from the late 1930s onwards to liquidate all Red Army Defence Areas on the country's western flank, as well as the lack of sufficiently strong forces in the new border areas incorporated into the state after the invasion of Poland almost two years earlier.

That same day, the leader of the French People's Party, Jacques Doriot, put forward a proposal to the occupation authorities to set up a unit of citizens of the conquered Third French Republic to participate in the expedition to secure living space (*lebensraum*) in the East. The next day, Marcel Déat, the leader of the National People's Assembly, met with the German ambassador to the French government, Otto Abetz. Fernand de Brinon, delegate of the Vichy French government, also supported the project. In early July 1941, German Foreign Minister Joachim von Ribbentrop approved the French collaborators' proposals. This event, which took place on 6 July, set in motion the epic of soldiers from France in the service of the *Wehrmacht*, and later the *Waffen-SS*. Interestingly, some of those who shortly after the outbreak of the war against the USSR declared their willingness to serve in the *Wehrmacht*, shed blood four years later in Pomerania.

LVF stamp from a letter sent in February 1943. (Studio Historyczne Huzar Archive)

Officially, the formation of the Legion of French Volunteers against Bolshevism (*Légion des volontaires française contre le bolschevisme*, or LVF) – the name given to the formation – began on 7 July 1941 with the establishment at the Majestic Hotel in Paris of the Legion Central Committee. It is curious to note that the hotel formerly housed a Soviet tourist agency. This act was actually contrary to current French law, which formally prohibited its citizens from serving under a foreign banner. Despite this, the approval of the creation of LVF was given by Marshal Pétain, who also headed the unit.[1]

On 5 August, the formation of the unit was officially proclaimed. Approximately 13,000 Frenchmen soon declared their willingness to join its ranks. Author Carlos Jurado wrote in 2002 that about 5,700 of these passed the initial verification; around 2,500 volunteers finally qualified for service.[2] It is worth noting that the announcement of recruitment to the LVF as an official part of the *Wehrmacht* met with extreme public reactions around France, with a large number of people strongly objecting. Some, despite the expected repression by the Nazis, dared to take radical action. For example, there was a failed assassination attempt on Vichy Prime Minister Pierre

---

1   D. Littlejohn, *Foreign Legions of...*, pp. 125–27.
2   C. Jurado, *Germany's Eastern Front...*, p. 6.

Laval and the Nazi sympathizers Jacques Doriot and Marcele Déat at Versailles on 27 August by Paul Collette, a veteran of the 1940 campaign.

The French volunteers were named the *Infanterieregiment 638*. The group was originally headed by a representative of the Vichy government with the German governor of Paris, General Joseph Louis François Hassler, and recruits were to be issued French Army uniforms of the type used at the beginning of hostilities in Western Europe. This decision to wear French uniforms was quickly changed due to the fact that, according to international law, as well as the regiment belonging to the armed forces of the Third Reich, such uniforms could not be used outside of France. The commander finally selected was a 61-year-old military historian, Colonel Roger Labonne.[3]

The first group of LVF recruits, which numbered 828 soldiers, of which 25 were officers (mainly of German origin), set off on 4 September 1941 to a training ground in Pustków near Dębica in Poland. Nine hundred more volunteers joined them a couple of weeks later. At the beginning of the following month, *Infanterieregiment 638* had almost 2,500 Frenchmen gathered in two battalions, command by 35 German officers.

LVF soldiers pose for propaganda purposes. This picture was published in *Signal* magazine. In 1945, the *tricolor* shield of France was used by the Legion veterans transferred to the *Waffen-SS*. (*Signal* Magazine)

3   D. Littlejohn, *Foreign Legions of...*, pp. 146–47.

LVF soldiers during the 1941 winter campaign. At that time the French unit was employed mainly with the German *7. Infanterie-Division* in its advance towards Moscow. (Bundesarchiv, Bild Bild 101I-141-1291-07, photo: Momber [top], Bild 101I-141-1291-08, photo: Momber [bottom])

The following month, the LVF was sent to the Eastern Front. The Legion reached Smolensk by rail, and then, using trucks provided by the *Wehrmacht*, they were moved to the village of Gołokowo. They made their debut in battle alongside the German *7. Infanterie-Division* of *Generalleutnant* Ecchart Freiherr von Gablenz during the attack on Moscow.[4] During this time, near Czestochowa in Kruszyn, the formation began of the third French battalion. Of this unit's 1,400 recruits, 200 were from French African colonies, among them Algerians and Arabs.[5] After suffering heavy losses in battles against the Red Army, *Infanterieregiment 638* was withdrawn to near the village of Diukowo until 9 December 1941. The second battalion remained outside the main line of operations until February 1942 and stood on the verge of being disbanded. The following month, Colonel Labonne was dismissed as commander of the LVF, with no successor appointed until June 1943, when the position was taken by Colonel (promoted to general in April 1944) Edgar Puaud from Orleans, a veteran of the First World War, graduate of the French Military Academy at St Cyr and recipient of the *Légion d'honneur*. In the meantime, the unit was split up, with the first battalion serving under the *186. Sicherungs-Division*. There was also at this time a struggle for more staff for the unit, which in the following weeks finally began to reach the territories occupied by the *Wehrmacht* in the USSR.[6]

In spring 1942, the LVF was reorganized, with two infantry battalions and three artillery batteries. The unit was used during operations against Soviet partisans, including around Bryansk, Mogilev and Orsha,[7] with its HQ based successively in Borysów, Smolensk and Kotów. On 28 June 1942, some sub-units were included in the theoretically independent formation that went under the name of the Tri-Color Legion (*Légion Tricolore*), initiated by the Secretary of State in the Vichy government, Jacques Benoit-Mechin. This experiment ultimately failed, with the associated recruitment campaign ended that October. By the middle of the following year, the second battalion was also reconstructed. On 27 August 1943, some soldiers returned to Paris to participate in celebrations for the first anniversary of the LVF. During these devents, all sub-units down to company level were given banners; in the case of the newly formed battalion, the slogan of the Foreign Legion, 'March or Die!', was embroidered on the flag.

The last year of the group's operation in the ranks of the *Wehrmacht* (1944) began with their inclusion in large-scale actions against Soviet partisans in Ukraine, under Operation Morocco. In June, the first battalion of the LVF was included in an improvised battlegroup in the vicinity of Bobruisk. With the support of two *Panzerkampfwagen VI* Tiger tanks, they halted constant Russian attacks for two days, becoming the basis of a legend later repeated in the ranks of the *33. Waffen-Grenadier*

---

4   R. Landwehr, *French Volunteers of the Waffen-SS* (Bennington: 2006).
5   D. Littlejohn, *Foreign Legions of...*, p. 149.
6   P.P. Lambert & G. Le Marec, *Les Français sous le casque allemand* (Paris: 2002), p. 7.
7   F. Steiner, *Ochotnicy Waffen-SS...*, p. 211.

An LVF soldier during the battle for Moscow in November or December 1941. A group of veterans of that campaign joined the *Charlemagne* Brigade, and then Divison in 1943. (Bundesarchiv, Bild 101I-214-0328-24, photo: Gebauer)

Division der SS Charlemagne. In the second half of July, the LVF was withdrawn to the region of Szczecin (Stettin).[8] Then on 1 September, General Puaud's men formally joined the ranks of the *Waffen-SS*.[9]

As determined by the author of an extensive monograph on foreign units in the Wehrmacht, David Littlejohn, other than the Legion of French Volunteers Against Bolshevism, only about 300 French citizens served in the German Army. Most of them were concentrated in the ranks of the *3. SS-Panzer-Division 'Totenkopf'* and *5. SS-Panzer-Division 'Wiking'*.[10] On 22 June 1943 – the second anniversary of the German invasion of the Soviet Union – the Committee of Friends of the *Waffen-SS* (*Comité des Amis de la Waffen-SS*) was created in Paris. Once again, the Hotel Majestic became the base of this organization, just like two years earlier for the LVF.[11] The task of this group, supervised by the Vichy Ministry of Information, was to look for candidates for service in the then-unnamed French *Waffen-SS* unit. After just two months, the French *SS*-Volunteer Grenadier Regiment (*Französische SS-Freiwilligen-Grenadier-Regiment*) was formed.

The 800-strong first group of volunteers who applied to the unit included 17-year-old Andre Bayle from Marseille. He later headed one of the battlegroups during the fighting in Ukraine. Initially, he was sent with his companions to the St Andreas training camp at Sennheim in Alsace. It turned out that, contrary to expectations, the

8   R. Landwehr, *French Volunteers...*, pp. 14–15.
9   D. Littlejohn, *Foreign Legions of...*, p. 155.
10   R. Landwehr, *French Volunteers...*, p. 9.
11   Ch. Hale, *Hitler's Foreign Executioners. Europe's Dirty Secret* (Stroud: 2011), p. 346.

instructors were not German officers, but Dutch and Flemish who had experience of fighting on the Eastern Front.

Recruitment was soon intensified. Among others, Vichy militia officers, members of the French Guard and Germans from Alsace and Lorraine began appearing in front of the enrollment commission, which was located at Avenue du Recteur Poincaré 24 in Paris. As author Christoph Bishop points out, those interested in serving in the regiment also included French-speaking inhabitants of Indochina, a group of Swedes, several Jews[12] and even one Japanese from Martinique[13]. At that time, attention was paid primarily to age – recruits had to be between 20 and 25 – and physical fitness. Joseph Darnand, who supervised the recruitment operation, was awarded the rank of *SS-Obersturmbannführer*.[14]

On 18 August, Hitler approved the creation of the French unit within the *Waffen-SS*. In November, 30 French officers who joined its ranks were sent on a course to the *SS-Junkerschule Bad Tölz* training school, while 100 future non-commissioned officers went to the *Waffen-Unterführerschule Posen-Treskau* establishment in Owińska near Poznań, Poland.

One of the French volunteers joining the *Waffen-SS* in Paris during the summer of 1943. (Bundesarchiv, Bild 101III-Apfel-017-30, photo: Apfel)

Before the eight companies grouped in two battalions of the *Französische SS-Freiwilligen-Grenadier-Regiment* managed to move to the front, the unit was transformed into the French *SS*-Volunteer Assault Brigade (*Französische SS-Freiwilligen Sturmbrigade*), which became the *SS*-Assault Brigade 'Frankreich' (*SS-Freiwilligen Sturmbrigade 'Frankreich'*)–. On 18 July 1944, it was decided to send the French units to the southern sector of the Eastern Front, which was by then in Polish territory. Twelve days later, a combat group of 1,800 men, formally

---

12   Ch. Bishop, *SS: Hell on the Western Front* (St Paul: 2003), p. 90.
13   D. Littlejohn, *Foreign Legions of...*, p. 170.
14   Ibid., p. 159.

appearing as the 1st Battalion of Frankreich (*I./Frankreich*), was transported through Czech territory to the Dukla Pass, where it was included in the *18. SS-Freiwilligen Panzergrenadier-Division 'Horst Wessel'*, commanded by *SS-Brigadeführer* Wilhelm Trabant. This unit was for the most part composed of ethnic Germans from Banat in the Balkans. Almost immediately after the arrival of transport, they set off as part of *Kampfgruppe Schäfe* built around the *40. SS-Panzergrenadier Regiment.* In the middle of the following month, the unit, by then commanded by *SS-Hauptsturmführer* Erich Kostenbader, was in retreat, reaching the area around Sanok and Mielec in south-east Poland. After escaping a trap prepared by the attacking Red Army, they moved to Sandomierz.

LVF soldiers during fighting on the Eastern Front in the winter of 1941/42. (Bundesarchiv, Bild 101I-141-1258-15, photo: Momber)

At this point, it is worth mentioning an episode recalled by Richard Landwehr in a book devoted to French volunteers fighting for Germany. On 19 August 1944, an *SS-Sturmbrigade 'Frankreich'* patrol ran into Soviet reconnaissance forces on the Vistula. Rather than fight, they took a bath in the river and exchanged personal items.[15] This was a very rare event, as every day the French participated in fierce battles, which resulted in losses of more than half of the original company. Nearly two-thirds of the

15   R. Landwehr, *French Volunteers...*, pp. 19–23.

men serving under *Waffen-Obersturmbannführer* Paul Gamory-Dubourdeau suffered severe wounds and seven out of 18 officers fit for action at the beginning of the month were killed, while eight were injured.[16]

On 23 August, the unit was moved to Tarnów-Dębica, from where it was evacuated via Gdańsk (Danzig) to the training ground at Chojnice (Konitz). From there, they were transported to Gryfice (Greifenberg) in Western Pomerania. There, out of the entire brigade, only some 140 had not suffer some wounds during the fighting. They were then joined by veterans of the LVF, who, on 1 September, were placed under the tutelage of the *SS*-Central Office.

During the group's reconstruction in the Gryfice barracks, information about the patron of the French unit appeared for the first time. Initially, it was supposed to be the heroine from the Hundred Years' War, the Maid of Orleans, Joan of Arc. However, it was thought that as a woman, she was not suitable for patronizing a unit of male fighters. The choice eventually fell on the legendary early ninth-century Holy Roman Emperor *Charlemagne*. At the time, a specific division of powers was established within the unit. The operational commander of the formation was verified as *Waffen-Oberführer* Edgar Puaud, assisted by a fluent French-speaking officer of the occupation staff in Paris, *SS-Brigadeführer* Gustav Krukenberg. At the same time, Jean-Marcel Renault was appointed as Franco–German liaison officer.

LVF soldiers somewhere in the Soviet Union, 1941/42. (Bundesarchiv, Bild 101I-214-0328-28, photo: Gebauer)

16   D. Littlejohn, *Foreign Legions of…*, p. 161.

On 26 October, the unit was moved again to the camp at Wildflecken in Lower Franconia, Bavaria, where the brigade's school and reserve battalion was created. They were commanded by the Swiss *Waffen-Obersturmbannführer* Heinrich Hersche. The nearby barracks at Bad Brückenau became the official base of the Frenchmen, and *SS-Sturmbannführer* Erich Lölhoffel and *SS-Sturmbannführer* Katzian led the two battalions forming the core of the unit.[17]

The stay in Bavaria was mainly used to fill staff shortages and to complete the re-equipping of the unit. Frenchmen who served the Third Reich in various different services began arriving to join their compatriots.

One of them who was later assigned to the headquarters company of the *Charlemagne* Division was Robert Soulat. In 1938, as an 18-year-old, he joined the ranks of the French Army, initially being assigned to an anti-tank company and then a heavy company of the second battalion of the 24th Tunisian Rifle Regiment. During the 1940 campaign in Western Europe, he participated in the battles on the Maas River and on 20 May was captured by the German *7. Panzer-Division*. He spent the next two-and-a-half years in POW camps, including at Żagań and Głogów. He was released in mid-February 1943 and returned to Paris, where he volunteered to work in a construction unit of *Einsatzgruppe Westen* of the Todt Organization. From there, at his own request, he joined the *Kriegsmarine* in May 1944. He was assigned to the 28th Navy Reserve Battalion (*28. Schiffstammabteilung*) at Duisburg in the Rhineland, from there being transferred to Gryfice and then Wildflecken with many of the other French volungteers. In a letter to the author of this book, written in early September 2011, he recalled:

> In September, the formation of the *Charlemagne* Brigade began, so we were directed to the training camp in Wildflecken. At the beginning, like the other former members of the *Kriegsmarine*, I went to the *Wach-und-Ausblidungs Company der Inspektion*, but because of my height (162cm) I was sent to the staff of the brigade staff. Fortunately, my quite good knowledge of German (six years of high school, three years in a prisoner of war camp, one year in the Todt Organization and four months in the *Kriegsmarine*) was noticed, so I was transferred to a group of translators for the German officers supervising the formation of the brigade."[18]

As part of their training, and often also for their first contact with weapons, some future officers were delegated to the *SS-Panzergrenadierschule* Kienschlag in Prosečnice, central Bohemia, and *SS-Truppenübungsplatz* Bohmen in the Protectorate of Bohemia and Moravia. In the first of these centres, *Waffen-Sturmbannführer* Cance worked as a liaison with the German commandant, while *Waffen-Obersturmbannführer* Paul

17   R. Landwehr, *French Volunteers...*, p. 33.
18   Letter of Robert Soulat to the author, 7 September 2011.

Gamory-Dubourdeau started work in the same role, but at the *SS*-Main Office in Berlin.[19] Referring to these events described, the commander of the *III (germanische) SS-Panzerkorps*, *SS-Obergruppenführer* Felix Steiner, stated: "For the first time in European history the French and Germans fought not against each other, but as comrades-in-arms ... The French took the side of the Germans against a common enemy of Europe. In this way, they overcame the age-old prejudice that until now brought only unhappiness to both nations."[20]

Waffen-Rottenführer Robert Soulat, from the *Charlemagne* Division HQ Company. This picture was taken during his service with Organization Todt in 1943. (Studio Historyczne Huzar Archive)

Although mention of an increase in the French unit's role under the *Waffen-SS* had been circulating within its ranks since early September 1944, *SS-Sturmbrigade Charlemagne* was only formally raised to division status probably on 10 November that year.[21] *SS-Brigadeführer* Krukenberg's men were not informed about this until 10 February 1945, although, according to their accounts, many only learned about it after the end of the Second World War.[22] The personnel of the branch, which received the official name of the 33rd *SS*-Grenadier Division *Charlemagne* (*33. Waffen-Grenadier-Division der SS Charlemagne*), were soon increased to 7,340 all ranks. As calculated by David Littlejohn, some 1,000 of them were veterans of the previous *SS*-Assault Brigade, including those who arrived after the fighting of the previous year, while 1,200 were former soldiers of the LVF, 2,500 were Vichy policemen and 640 were Frenchmen who had served in the *Kriegsmarine*.[23]

19 *33. Waffen-Grenadier-Division der...*, p. 7.
20 F. Steiner, *Ochotnicy Waffen-SS...*, p. 212.
21 R. Landwehr, *French Volunteers...*, pp. 31–34.
22 R. Forbes, *For Europe. The French Volunteers of the Waffen-SS* (Solihull: 2006), p. 240.
23 D. Littlejohn, *Foreign Legions of...*, p. 190.

Waffen-Rottenführer Robert Soulat
during his service in the *28.
Schiffstammabteilung* in Swinemünde.
(Private archive)

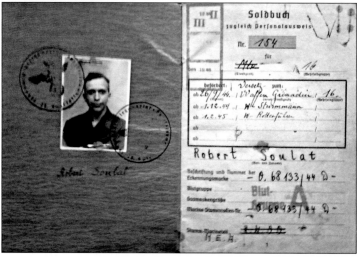

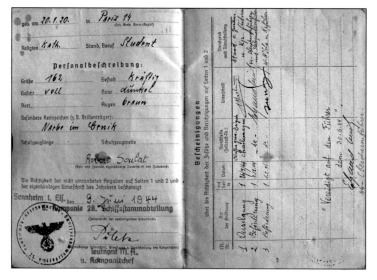

Most of them joined with the atmosphere prevailing within the unit, even before it was moved to the front. As recalled by those who were there, in Wildflecken a kind of hero cult emerged around the field commanders who had shown extraordinary courage and ability during the battles of the *SS-Sturmbrigade 'Frankreich'*. The highest esteem was given to the head of the newly formed 1st battalion of the 57th *SS*-Grenadier Regiment (*57. Waffen-Grenadier Regiment der SS*), *Waffen-Hauptsturmführer* Henri Fenet, and commander of the 2nd battalion, *Waffen-Obersturmführer* Ivan Bartolomei.[24] The fighting spirit was also influenced by the chaplain of the division and the LVF, the Parisian Father Jean de Mayol de Lupè, about whom. Christian la Mazière, who joined the *Charlemagne* Brigade in August 1944, remarked after the war:

> He was like a knight, like a monk fighting like the crusaders of the past, raising a crucifix over the battlefield, and if that was not enough – with sword that cut off heads. The only thing that made him different from them was the revolver in place of the sword. He reminded people of the Renaissance, not so much because of his uncontrollable temperament, but thanks to his sophistication and huge culture. The zeal of the crusader combined with his charisma ... It was impossible not to smile at the thought of this charming, yet dual character, whose virtuosity and indisputable honesty multiplied his faces. He came from an extremely old and respectable family and lived among us in his own old-fashioned world."[25]

The division was composed of two grenadier regiments: the 57th, commanded by *Waffen-Hauptsturmführer* Victor de Bourmont, including the 33rd *SS*-Reserve Company, and the 58th, led by *Waffen-Sturmbannführer* Emile Raybaud (formerly *Waffen-Sturmbannführer* Jeana Bridouksa). There were also the 33rd *SS*-anti tank battalion (*Waffen-Sturmbannführer* Jean Boudet-Gheusi), 33rd *SS*-artillery battalion (*Waffen-Hauptsturmführer* Jean Havette) and the following independent companies: signals (*Waffen-Obersturmführer* Jean Dupuyau), engineers (*Waffen-Obersturmführer* de Vitrolles), and 57th *SS*-military police platoon (*Waffen-Obersturmführer* Guillaume Veyrieras).[26]

A battery of assault guns was assigned to the anti-tank squadron, commanded by *Waffen-Obersturmführer* Pierre Michel. Originally, it was to be equipped with *Sturmgeschütz 40* or *Jagdpanzer 38(t) Hetzer* vehicles. According to historian David Littlejohn, the French were informed that the unit would be equipped with heavy tanks in the future.[27] In fact, their crews acted as ordinary infantry.[28]

24   J. Trigg, *Hitler's Gauls: The History of the 33rd Waffen Division Charlemagne* (Staplehurst: 2006), p. 76.
25   C. De La Mazière, *Marzyciel w...*, pp. 38–39.
26   I. Baxter, *Ostatnie lata Waffen-SS* (Warsaw: 2010), p. 195.
27   D. Littlejohn, *Foreign Legions of...*, p. 172.
28   J. Mabire, *Mourir á Berlin* (Paris: 1997), p. 90.

The absence of tracked vehicles, which the division never received, was not the only shortage that the French soldiers had to deal with. If you believe the combination of forces and resources of the unit which were preserved in the collections of the *Bundesarchiv-Militärarchiv* in Freiburg (Breisgau), only three *Steyr Raupenschlepper Ost* tractors, three half-track tractors and 44 trucks were available for divisional HQ.[29] The condition of the artillery was no better: just three 7.5cm *Panzerabwehrkanone 40* and 5cm *Panzerabwehrkanone 38* anti-tank guns, five 15cm *Schwereinfanteriegeschütz 33* heavy infantry guns, eight 10.5cm *Leichtefeldhaubitze 18* light field howitzers, 12 7.5cm *Infanteriegeschütz 18* light infantry guns and nine 3.7cm *Flugabwehrkanone 18/36/37/43* anti-aircraft guns. In addition, there were 872 disposable anti-tank *Panzerfausts* and 72 reusable 8.8cm *Raketenpanzerbüchse 43* or *54*.[30] There was also a lack of uniforms and individual equipment, including coats or other winter clothing,[31] and even steel helmets.

29   Robert Soulat testimony preserved in the author's private archive, p. 13.
30   Bundesarchiv-Militärarchiv Freiburg, doc. B-15/Ia/F/15/2.
31   According to Robert Soulat testimony (author's archive), some *Charlemagne* Division soldiers had been equipped with brown NSDAP or SA tunics.

3

Destination Pomerania

On 12 January 1945, the Red Army, supported by the First Polish Army, launched the Vistula–Oder Operation. The first stage, a massed attack across the Vistula, surprised both the civil and military authorities of the Third Reich, as well as the attackers themselves in its success. On the fourth day of the operation, the Chief of Staff of the *Wehrmacht* Supreme Command, *Generalleutnant* August Winter, reported that German forces in occupied Poland had virtually lost all defensive capability. At that time, the Soviet 2nd Guards Tank Army commanded by General Semyon Bogdanow, which was part of the 1st Belorussian Front heading directly to Berlin, covered a distance of 300km and reached Bydgoszcz (Bromberg during the German occupation of Poland). On 22 January, the spearhead of the 9th Guards Tank Corps breached the Noteć River, capturing an intact bridge near Nakło (Nakel an der Netze). The road into Pomerania was now open.

The defence of the Province of Pomerania (*Provinz Pommern*), the area bounded by the cities of Stralsund, Demmin, Neustrelitz and Łeba (Leba) Bytów (Bütow), Bobolice (Bublitz) and Okonek (Ratzebuhr in Pommern), had been organized by the local the community in the belief that there was no danger of the Red Army appearing in its territory. Although there had been some feverish fortification-building since the summer of 1944, which resulted in the preparation of potential defence positions, hardly anyone believed such a rapid development of events that followed shortly thereafter was likely. A three-phase alarm project to protect Pomerania against the enemy from the east was created, under the code name Gneisenau – referring to General August von Gneisenau, the legendary defender of Kołobrzeg against the *Grande Armée* of Napoleon Bonaparte. The first stage was Operation Rain (Regen), which involved preparing German property for evacuation west or north across the Baltic Sea. Operation Grad (Hagel), the second stage, was the export to safe places in the Third Reich of resources and movable production plants. The last stage, Operation Snow (Schnee), involved a massive outflow of civilians. In December 1944, matters relating to the above procedures, previously approved by the commander of the

2nd Military District (*Wehrkreis II*), General Werner Kienitz, were sent to all local government officials.

Due to the rapid advance of the Soviet and Polish forces, on Saturday, 20 January 1945, around 1800 hours local time, the Gneisenau alarm was finally rung.[1] Along with the hasty and chaotic evacuation of civilians, often preceded by the flight of regional dignitaries – who coordinated the whole project to the very end – thirty-third mobilization of military mobilization was launched in the history the Third Reich. The same day, the formation began of improvised divisional groups: *Einsatz Division Bärwalde* (in Barwice, commanded by Generalleutnant Wilhelm Raithel), *Einsatz Division Köslin* (Koszalin, *Oberst* Peter Sommer), *Einsatz Division Märkisch-Friedland* (Mirosławiec, *Oberst* Kurt Lehmann) and *Einsatz Division Woldenberg* (Dobiegniew, *Generalmajor* Gerhard Kegler). All soldiers on leave in the region were included in the ad hoc units. *Volkssturm* formations were also called into service. They consisted mostly of inhabitants of the areas they were to defend, which was the core of their mostly poor *esprit de corps*. There was also a hasty replenishment of those units guarding the borders of the Pomeranian Position (*Pommernstellung*), the belt of fortifications built in the early 1930s. The first columns of refugees appeared on the region's roads, which caused considerable difficulties in the dislocation of newly created armed formations.[2]

Two days after Red Army troops crossed the Noteć to launch the Pomeranian campaign, the Army Group Vistula (*Heeresgruppe Weichsel*) was founded on 24 January, headed by the head of the Reserve Army and *Reichsführer-SS*, Heinrich Himmler.[3] The task of the staff of the new army group, whose first headquarters was at Piła (Schneidemühl), was to fill the gap between Army Group A and Army Group Centre as soon as possible, preventing the enemy from striking in the direction of Gdańsk, Greater Poland with Poznań and the east bank of the Oder. Then, in a completely unachievable plan, units of *Heeresgruppe Weichsel*, were to start a counterattack to merge with German units operating in Lower Silesia. On the day thayt*Reichsführer-SS* Himmler's staff was constituted, the Russians broke the *Wehrmacht*'s defences in the Olsztyn and Iława regions, crossing the western part of the pre-war border of East Prussia. The fighting then moved to the vicinity of Malbork and Elbląg, threatening Pomerania not only, as originally assumed, from the south, but also the east, which was protected by the *Pommernstellung*.[4] *Heeresgruppe Weichsel*'s staff could only field 25 outdated tanks against the advancing enemy swarms, along with 35 assault guns – which probably included Marder III tank destroyers – and 12 88mm anti-tank

1   W. Kienitz, *Der Wehrkreis II vor dem Zusammenbruch des Reiches* (Hamburg: 1955), p. 27.
2   Ł. Gładysiak, *Alarm na Pomorzu Zachodnim*, [w:] 'Głos Kołobrzegu', 20 January 2012, Koszalin, p. 15.
3   H. Lindenblatt, *Pommern 1945. Eines der letzten Kapitel in der Geschichte vom Untergant des Dritten Reiches* (Würzburg: 2008), p. 30.
4   *Die Wehrmachtsberichte 1939–1945. Band 3: 1. Januar 1944 bis 9. Mai 1945. Orts-, Personen- und Formationsregister* (Köln: 1989), p. 415.

guns. First-line units were given only about 100 trucks, and there were no sub-units protecting the facilities.[5]

Foreign *Waffen-SS* units were directed to man the defences in Pomerania, under the *XVI SS-Armeekorps* commanded by *SS-Obergruppenführer* Karl-Maria Demelhuber. On the eve of the formation of Army Group Vistula, it included the 15th *SS*-Grenadier Division of the Latvian Army (*15. Waffen-Grenadier Division der SS lettische Nummer 1*), often completely incorrectly called the Lettland Division, which numbered at this time about 17,000 men,[6] and directed from the vicinity of Ujście (Utz) and Piła, the Dutch *48. SS-Panzergrenadier Regiment General Seyffardt*. Initially, their units manned a foothold on the Noteć River, in the Nakło (Nakel an der Netze) and Bydgoszcz region, with the spearhead for the planned counterattack created by Latvian citizens under the command of *SS-Oberführer* Herbert von Obwurzer.[7] A second defensive line was designated for them, which was located on the Blücher Line (*Blücher-Stellung*), a network of field fortifications prepared in summer and autumn 1944 and extending from Ustka (Stolpmünde) and Słupsk (Stolp).[8] In addition, the *16. SS-Armeekorps* included the following formations: the *32. Infanterie-Division*, called the Lion's Head (*Löwenkopf*) Division, formed in the mid-1930s and whose sub-units were intended to defend the central part of the Pomeranian Province before the outbreak of war; the *59. Grenadier Regiment*; the improvised *Kampfgruppe Wagner*; and a separate *Regiment Hammerstein*.[9]

On the last day of January, advance elements of the Soviet 8th Mechanized Guards Corps stood near Kostrzyn on the Oder. This created the so-called Pomeranian salient, the liquidation of which the Stavka – the leadership of the Supreme Command

5   *Tagebuch Nr 768/45. Heeresgruppe Weichsel. Anlagen zum Kriegstagebuch 21.1.45–31.1.45*, United States National Archives, T311 Roll 167.

6   Ł. Gładysiak, *Przełamanie Wału Pomorskiego. Działania 1. Armii Wojska Polskiego od 30 stycznia do 11 lutego 1945 r.*, [w:] 'Militaria XX wieku. Wydanie Specjalne', nr 1(17) (Lublin: 2011), p. 10.

7   *Abschrift A 24/3. Heeresgruppe Weichsel. Anlagen zum Kriegstagebuch 21.1.45–31.1.45*, United States National Archive, T311 Roll 167. As early as 23 January 1945, soldiers of the *15. SS-Grenadier Division* participated in the successful freeing of around 1,000 prisoners in Mroczy (Immenheim). Subunits of this formation then joined the hastily formed battlegroup in the Nakło area (Nakel an der Netze) along with the reinforced Dutch *48. SS-Panzergrenadier Regiment*, a mixed division of the Gross Born motorized artillery and elements of the 325th anti-aircraft battery, which had 88mm guns. In the following days, these units participated, among others, in battles against the 1st Polish Army at Złotów (Flatow), Podgaje (Flederborn) and Jastrów (Jastrow). *Abschrift A 24/8. Befehl für die Verteidigung des Netze-Abschnittes Nr. 1. Heeresgruppe Weichsel. Anlagen zum Kriegstagebuch 21.1.45–31.1.45*, United States National Archives, T311 Roll 167, and *Abschrift B 3/10. Fernspruch von Ingrid Alt 3.2. 17,45 Uhr, Heeresgruppe Weichsel. Anlagen zum Kriegstagebuch 1.2.45–14.2.45*, United States National Archives, T311 Roll 167.

8   H. Lindenblatt, *Pommern 1945…*, p. 103.

9   *Morgensmeldung vom 31.1.1945, Heeresgruppe Weichsel. Anlagen zum Kriegstagebuch 21.1.45–31.1.45*, United States National Archives, T311 Roll 167.

of the Red Army – entrusted to the Soviet 47th and 61st Armies, supported by the 2nd Tank Army and the 1st Polish Army.[10] The advance guarde of the latter, the 1st Infantry Division of Tadeusz Kościuszko and the 4th Infantry Division of Jan Kiliński, launched its attack on 29 January 29, having the previous day crossed the pre-war Polish–German border at Dorotowo. During subsequent fighting they reached Złotów (Flatow). At the same time, the Soviet 2nd Guards Cavalry Corps advanced on the Jastrowie (Jastrow) to Podgaje (Flederborn) line, where the main forces of the German *XVI SS-Armeekorps* were concentrated.[11] By breaking the *SS* corps' defences here, and the Polish 12th Infantry Regiment occupying the town of Szwecja (Freudenfier) near Wałcz (Deutsch Krone), the Red Army was in position for the final breakthrough to the *Pommernstellung* in the first week of February on the section Nadarzyce (Rederitz)–Golce (Neugolz)–Zdbice (Stabitz).[12]

With formations of *Heeresgruppe Weichsel* in such an unfavourable position, Berlin decided, on 2 February, to launch a mass counterattack to defeat the Soviet bridgeheads across the Oder, extending from the vicinity of Stargard (Stargard in Pommern) and Choszczno (Arnswalde) to Lower Silesia. Implementation of the project, which was initially codenamed Operation Hussar Charge (*Unternehmen Husarenritt*), and finally Operation Solstice (*Unternehmen Sonnenwende*),[13] rested on the shoulders of the staff of the *11. SS-Panzerarmee* commanded by *SS-Obergruppenführer* Felix Steiner. On 9 February, consent was given to the formation of an attack force including *Panzer Division Holstein*, *III SS-Panzerkorps* under the command of *Generalleutnant* Martin Unrein, who had just been designated for this post – composed of the *11. SS-Panzergrenadier Division 'Nordland'* with national regiments of volunteers from Denmark and Norway, the Dutch *23. SS-Panzergrenadier Division 'Nederland'*, the Flemish *27. SS-Grenadier Division 'Langemarck'* and the *Führer-Begleit Division* – and the *28. SS-Division 'Wallonien'*.

The same day, however, the attacking group was weakened by the delegating of the last of these units, along with the *10. SS-Panzer Division 'Frundsberg'* and the *4. SS-Polizei Division*, under the command of *Generalleutnant* Karl Decker's *XXXIX Panzerkorps*. According to the original plans, the counterattack was to take place on 15 February, with forces deployed in three sections. In the west were the units of *Generalleutnant* Decker, who were to advance from Stargard, through the isthmus between lakes Miedwie and Płoń, to Pyrzyce (Pyritz). In the east, the *281. Infanterie-Division* of *Generalleutnant* Bruno Ortner and the *Führer-Grenadier Division*, and the rest of *Korpsgruppe Münzel* under *Generalmajor* Oskar Münzel, were placed against the Red Army. Support was also provided by soldiers of the *402. Ersatz*

10   There were 93,000 soldiers in the 1st Polish Army at this time, some 73,000 of whom were gathered in front-line formations.
11   Ł. Gładysiak *Przełamanie Wału…*, p. 11.
12   Ibid., pp. 16–17.
13   Ibid.,p. 4.

Division, which was specifically excluded for this purpose from the structure of the *X SS-Armeekorps*. Between them was placed the already mentioned *III SS-Panzerkorps* of *Generalleutnant* Unrein, tasked with rescuing the units under *Generalmajor* Hans Voigt from Choszczno. It is worth noting that virtually none of the above entities were full-time formations. An additional weakness was the shortage of tracked vehicles. For this reason, *Panzerkampfwagen VI Ausführung B* heavy tanks – better known today as Royal or King Tigers – belonging to the *schwere SS-Panzerabteilung 503* proved to be an important asset, especially in the first days of the counterattack. The first four tanks arrived in late January and early February around Choszczno from Drawno (Neuwedell), 25km away, and another 11 arrived on 4 February from Suchań (Zachan).[14]

On 9 February, in preparation for the main part of the attack, German units began operations in the Lake Miedwie-Ina sector. Their priority objective, in addition to stopping further progress of the Red Army, which could have discovered the concentration of troops for use in *Unternehmen Sonnenwende*, was to regain control of the road junction at Lubiatów (Lindberg), 13km east of Pyrzyce. A day later, units of the *III. SS-Panzerkorps* struck at Recz (Reetz), temporarily ejecting troops of the Soviet 9th Guards Tank Corps.[15] In fighting lasting several hours, *Waffen-SS* forces helped ease their equipment shortages by capturing 11 Soviet 76.2mm ZiS-3 anti-tank guns and five 122mm M38 howitzers. On 11 February, Flemish troops from the *27. SS-Grenadier Division 'Langemarck'* were deployed to new positions near the village of Wapnica (Ravenstein), located on what is nowadays National Road 10. Despite local successes, Soviet pressure on positions occupied by the *11. SS-Panzerarmee* did not diminish. The garrison at Choszczno was also still surrounded, its situation getting worse by the hour. Consequently, the decision was taken to step up the counterattack. On 11 February, Unrein received a report about the combat readiness of the units subordinated to him,[16] confirming the plan of action 24 hours later. Soldiers took their final starting positions.

The offensive in the Stargard area began on 15 February, with the *11. SS-Panzergrenadier Division 'Nordland'* crossing the Ina River, which created a bridgehead about 3km south of Suchań.[17] The Danish *24. SS-Regiment* formed the spearhead, immediately followed by the *Führer-Begleit Division* armoured personnel carriers and the assault guns of the *11. SS-Panzer Abteilung Hermann von Salza*, supported by *SS-Panzerjäger Abteilung 11*. A moment later, the Dutch from the *23.*

14 P. Brzeziński, *Ocena szans operacji zaczepnej o kryptonimie 'Sonnenwende' na podstawie analizy możliwości niemieckich wojsk pancernych w końcowym etapie II wojny światowej. Luty 1945*, pomorze1945.com/file.php?file=17 (22.08.2012 r.), pp. 4–7.

15 *Morgensmeldung 10.2.45, Heeresgruppe Weichsel. Anlagen zum Kriegstagebuch 1.2.45– 14.2.45*, United States National Archives, T311 Roll 167.

16 *Abschrift B 14/6. Heeresgruppe Weichsel. Anlagen zum Kriegstagebuch 1.2.45–14.2.45*, United States National Archives, Mikrofilm T311 Roll 167.

17 *Tagesmeldung vom 15.2.45…*, s. 1.

SS-Panzergrenadier Division 'Nederland' joined the attack. Over the next 24 hours, soldiers of the *11. SS-Panzergrenadier Division 'Nordland'* managed to break the ring around Choszczno, enabling civilians to leave the city.[18]

Contrary to the offensive's intentions, the above events had only a local dimension. On 20 February, it became clear that joining the forces of *Heeresgruppe Weichsel* with German units grouped in today-s southwestern Poland was impossible. On the same day, the Soviet air force carried out a massive attack on Szczecin, which became a symbol of the crushing advantage of Germany's opponents. Three days later, *Sonnenwende* was cancelled and the units participating in it, counting their losses, returned to their starting positions. The Red Army did not slow its attack. At this time, the *33. Waffen-Grenadier Division der SS Charlemagne* was already being transferred to the front line, where it was to strengthen the Herresgruppe Weichsel in the central part of the Pomeranian salient. It would start its combat operations no later than 24 February.[19]

The *Charlemagne*, commanded by *SS-Brigadeführer* Gustav Krukenberg, was formally assigned to the staff of the *XVIII Gebirgskorps* (Mountain Corps) under the command of *General der Infanterie* Friedrich Hochbaum, whose staff at that time was very close to the front line in Rzeczenica (Stegers), near Człuchów (Schlochau), which had been occupied by the Germans since 1939. The formation arrived in Pomerania from Lapland on 15 February. Members of the *Charlemagne* were packed into about a dozen rail transportsand moved from Gryfice through Miastko (Rummelsburg) to Czarne, less than 20km west of Szczecinek (Neustettin). Defensive positions around this town constituted one of the key resistance points of the so-called Szczecin corridor, which stretched to the intersection of the operational areas of the Soviet 1st and 2nd Belorussian Fronts. Holding the area allowed other *Wehrmacht* units to reach this section of the front. The vanguard of the *Charlemagne* was the staff of *SS-Oberführer* Edgar Puaud. It included a German inspector, *SS-Standartenführer* Walther Zimmermann, later the commander of the *Charlemagne*, who was delegated from the ranks of the *7. SS-Freiwilligen Gebirgs-Division 'Prinz Eugen'*, , as well as elements of the unformed 33rd anti-tank battalion of *Waffen-Sturmbannführer* Boudet-Gheusi.

Events accompanying the expedition to Pomerania did not auger well. On 20 February, in the vicinity of Dąbie (Altdamm), the unit was shelled by the Soviet air force, resulting in the deaths of at least four Frenchmen. A few hours later, during a stop in Goleniów (Gollnow), the group was informed about their destination, Czarne. The soldiers arrived there early on 22 February at about 0200 hours local

---

18 *Morgensmeldung vom 17.2.45, Heeresgruppe Weichsel. Anlagen zum Kriegstagebuch 15.2.45–28.2.45,* United States National Archives, T311 Roll 168.

19 It is worth mentioning that the French formation appeared in official documents as the brigade, not division (*Französische SS-Freiwilligen Brigade*). *Tagesmeldung vom 21.2.45, Heeresgruppe Weichsel. Anlagen zum Kriegstagebuch 15.2.45–28.2.45,* United States National Archives, T311 Roll 168.

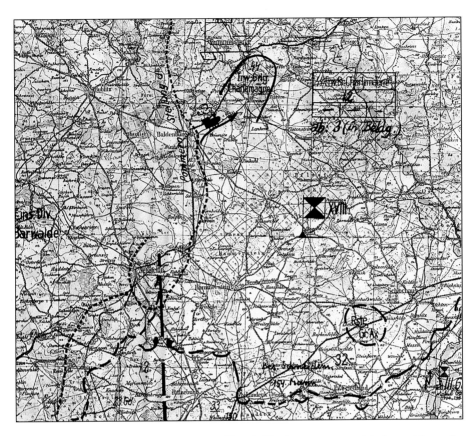

Part of an original German Army Group Vistula Headquarters map with the positions of *33. Waffen-Grenadier Division der SS Charlemagne* between from 23–26 February 1945. It appeared as a brigade at that time. (United States National Archives)

time. That morning, the 3rd and 4th companies of the *57. Grenadier Regiment der SS* arrived. The place of their concentration was a former prisoner-of-war camp, in which, to both side's surprise, a group of French POWs were encountered from the 1940 campaign. The first combat briefing was organized shortly after midnight on 23 February.[20] A few hours later, the regiment's 2nd company and a group of staff officers of the 2nd battalion with *Waffen-Hauptsturmführer* René André Obitz reached the future battlefield The following morning, the next echelon rolled into Hammerstein, carrying elements of *Grenadier–Abteilung 1* of the *58. Grenadier Regiment der SS* under the command of *Waffen-Sturmbannführer* Emile Raybaud. By 1700 hours, two more trains transporting the 1st, 2nd and 9th companies of the regiment had also arrived.

20   R. Forbes, *For Europe…*, pp. 249–50.

On 25 February, another group of soldiers, this time belonging to the divisional battalion of sappers, went not to Czarne but to Szczecinek. At the same time, five new Soviet divisions from Finland reached the front around Człuchów and Chojnice. The leading group of the Soviet 3rd Tank Corps under the command of General Nikolai Wiedenew was directed against the French positions.[21] The Soviet advantage in personnel and equipment was now overwhelming.

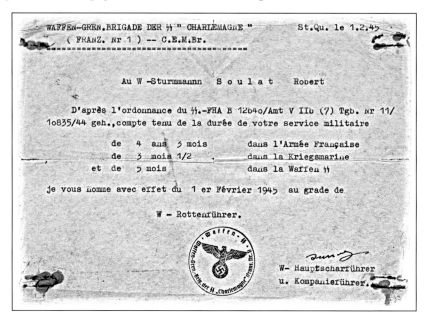

Robert Soulat's certificate of promotion to *Waffen-Rottenführer* (Lance Corporal), issued on 1 February 1945, just before the *Charlemagne* arrived in Pomerania. (Private archive)

On the morning of 24 February, Krukenberg called a staff meeting at the POW camp. As Robert Forbes has determined, the meeting was certainly attended by *Waffen-Oberführer* Puaud, *SS-Standartenführer* Zimmermann, *Waffen-Sturmbannführer* Raybaud, *Waffen-Sturmbannführer* Jean de Vaugelas and *Waffen-Hauptsturmführer* de Bourmont. They were informed that positions held so far by the German *32. Infanterie-Division* and the Latvian *15. SS-Grenadier Division* had been broken, and therefore their units should immediately prepare for battle. At this time, there were some 4,500 Frenchmen available to defend the section of the front between Czarne

21   A. Sroga, *Na drodze stał Kołobrzeg* (Warsaw: 1980), p. 25.

and Człuchów[22] (according to a statement preserved in the *Bundesarchiv-Militärarchiv* at Freiburg, the *33. Waffen-Grenadier Division der SS Charlemagne* had a combat readiness in February 1945 of 6,363 soldiers, including 102 officers and 856 NCOs[23]). The meeting also resulted in the establishing of key posts for maintaining positions. One of them, located on one of the region's main roads (today's National Road 22) at Uniechów (Heinrichswalde), commanded by *Waffen-Obersturmführer* Henri Fenet, was to be filled by soldiers of the 1st battalion of the *57. Grenadier Regiment der SS*. The area around Barkowo (Barkenfelde) was held by elements of the 2nd battalion under the command of *Waffen-Hauptsturmführer* Obitz. Temporarily subordinated to the staff of the *57. Regiment*, soldiers of the 1st battalion of the *58. Grenadier Regiment der SS* were allocated defence of the town of Biernatka (Bärenhütte), where it was also decided to transfer the command. The regiment's 2nd battalion was to be the division's reserve. The whole was to work closely with the *32. Infanterie-Division*, which was withdrawn in the vicinity of Czarne.

It should be assumed that the staff of the *33. Waffen-Grenadier-Division der SS Charlemagne* were aware that it would probably be impossible to fulfill the instructions of the staff of the *XVIII Gebirgskorps* without the support of heavy weapons. The situation was not improved by the diverse scope of small arms possessed by the troops, which became a characteristic feature of the formation throughout its fighting in Pomerania. As pointed out in correspondence with the author by *Waffen-Rottenführer* (Lance Corporal) Soulat, in addition to the standard types of German weapons – including 7.92mm *Mauser 98k* rifles and 9mm *Maschinenpistole 40* submachine guns – the troops had a small number of 7.92mm *Gewehr 43* rifles, French 7.5mm *MAS 36* carbines, Italian 9mm *Beretta wz. 1938* machine guns (according to the accounts of one of the soldiers, Jean-Paule Lefevre, this type of weapon was mainly in the hands of former officers of the Vichy militia) and a wide range of handguns, such as the 11.43mm US firearms taken during fighting in France, Colt wz. 1911 and Smith & Wesson revolvers. Some of the men had 7.62mm submachine guns, including the PPSz wz. 1941, well-known to veterans of the LVF. Such diversity obviously made it difficult to supply ammunition to the units. Basic equipment such as infantry knives, helmets and winter clothing were also missing.[24]

---

22 E. Lefèvre, *Charlemagne meurt sur l'Oder. Les combats de la division française des Waffen-SS en Poméranie Orientale – Février – Mars 1945*, [w:] 'Batailles. Histoire Militaire du XXᵉ Siècle', No. 6 (Paris: 2005), p. 53.

23 Bundesarchiv-Militärarchiv Freiburg, sygnatura B-15/Ia/F/15/2.

24 *Waffen-Rottenführer* Robert Soulat mentioned that he did not have a helmet when he reached Czarny. He only had a masking cover, which he later used as an additional head protection against the cold. He equipped himself with a field cap, probably of the type *Feldmütze 43*, only in April 1945, when, in Berlin, the *Charlemagne* intercepted a wrecked transport probably belonging to the *5. SS-Panzer Division 'Viking'* or the *11. SS-Grenadier Division 'Nordland'*. In addition, it is noteworthy that the French used insignia in the form of a three-colour shield, which was usually sewn on the left sleeve of uniforms. As revealed by analysis of archival photographs, this appeared most often just below the emblem of

D 29/1   (30)   01   24.2.45

Tagesmeldung

an O K H

Feindbild und Feindeindruck vor Oderfront der Heeresgruppe unverändert. Örtliche Angriffe des Gegners südlich des Madüsee, anscheinend mit dem Ziel, den vorgeschobenen Stützpunkt Pyritz von seinen rückwärtigen Verbindungen abzuschneiden. Erkannte Bewegungen im Raum nordwestlich Neuwedell (vor X.SS-A.K.) deuten auf Ablösung und Umgruppierung hin.

An Front 2. Armee setzte der Gegner seine Angriffe an den bisherigen Schwerpunkten gegen die Südfront der Armee fort, trat jedoch mit frisch herangeführten Kräften (Teile von 5 Divisionen der 19. Armee aufgetreten) gegen 32. Inf.Div. zwischen Marienfelde und nordwestlich Konitz zum Angriff an. Hauptsächlich mit Infanterie, unterstützt von Panzergruppen, gelang es dem Feind die Front zwischen Marienfelde und Janznick, das nach zähem Kampf in eigener Hand blieb, aufzureißen und mit seinen Angriffsspitzen nach Überschreiten des Haaken-Abschnittes bis in Gegend nördlich Heinrichswalde und 2 km südlich Bischofswalde durchzustoßen und damit die ursprüngliche Absicht der Armee, am Haaken-Abschnitt sich vorzulegen, zu vereiteln.

Die Armee ist daher gezwungen mit den noch einzeln Widerstand leistenden schwachen Kampfgruppen sowie den eingetroffenen Teilen der SS-Freiw.Brigade Charlemagne eine neue Abwehrfront in Linie Vangerow - Krummensee - Bischofswalde - Miskendorf aufzubauen. Gleichfalls brach Gegner mit Panzern nordwestlich Konitz in Richtung Großkornlage ein. Im Einbruchsraum Wespen

- 2 -

- 4 -

Südteil Leutmannsdorf verloren. Eigene Gegenangriffe hier, sowie gegen nordwestlich Gogeln eingebrochene Feindteile noch im Gange. An übriger Armeefront keine wesentliche Kampftätigkeit.

Starke Feindangriffe nach Trommelfeuer gegen Stellungen der Festung Graudenz am Süd- und Ostrand der Stadt. Sämtliche Angriffe unter erheblichen Feindverlusten bis auf eine geringfügige Einbruchsstelle, zu deren Bereinigung Gegenangriff im Gange, abgeschlagen. Starker Artillerie-Munitionsmangel.

2.) Nach Karte 1 : 300 000 durchgegeben.

3.) Herausgelöste Teile Pz.-Div."Holstein" Pz.A.O.K.3 unmittelbar unterstellt. (2 Btle. 281 J.D. zu Pz.-Div."Holstein").
1 Btl. und 1 Art.-Abt.10.SS-Pz.Div. zu SS-Div."Nordland".
10.SS-Pz.-Div. Pz.A.O.K.3 unmittelbar.
Regiment Jäckel und Regiment Riedel (Versprengten-Regiment) zu Div. "Pommerland".
Sturmgeschütz-Brigade 226 zu XVIII.Geb.-Korps.
33.SS-Brigade Charlemagne zu XVIII. Geb.-Korps.
Reste Pionier-Sperr-Brigade 1 zu 389.J.D.
A.A.München zu 4.Pz.Division.

4.) Volks-Artillerie-Korps 408 in Umgruppierung in Abschnitt XI. SS-Pz.-Korps.
Geplanter Versammlungsraum: Pz.Div."Holstein"; Raum südostwärts Sydowsaue und Raum hart nordwestlich Madüsee.
281.J.D. mit Masse Raum südwestlich Stargard eingetroffen.
2 Bataillone der Division bei Ablösung von 2 Batl. Pz.Div. "Holstein".
33.SS-Brigade Charlemagne beim Aufbau einer Riegelstellung von nördlich Krumensee bis zum Seonriegel nordostwärts davon.
Neuer Versammlungsraum 215. J.D. um und südwestlich Berent.
SS-Regiment Kaltofen (XXXIII. A.K. unterstellt)
- 5 -

- 5 -

im Raum Peplin.
Schwere Pz.Abt. 502 Raum um Swareschin.
Antransport:
33.SS-Brigade Charlemagne: 2 Züge (Stabskp.,und 4 Kompanien SS-Gren.Rgt.58).
215.J.D.: 5 Transporte
4.Pz.Div.: 1 Transport
Abgefahren:
Führer-Begl.-Div.: 10 Züge (Reste Art.Rgt.,II.Pz.Rgt., I.Pz.Rgt., Div.-Stab, Teile Nachschubtruppen).
4.Pol.-Div.: 7 Züge (Teile Pz.Abt., Teile Nachr.-Abt., Pi.-Batl., Teile San.-Abt.).
Führer-Gren.-Div.: 8 Züge (Teile Nachr.Abt., Div.-Stab, I.SS.Gren.-Rgt., Teile Füs.Batl., Teile Sturm-Art., Teile Rgt.-Stab Gren.Rgt., Feld-Ers.-Btl.).
10.SS-Pz.Div.: 9 Züge (Teile AA., Teile I.Pz.Abt., Teile Pi.-Btl., Teile Pz.Rgt., 1 San.-Kp.).
XXXIX.Pz.Korps: 4 Züge,(Teile Nachr.Abt., Führungsstab, Arko, V.P., Lfs.-Kp.)
5.)A.O.K. 11 auf Marsch nach Neustrelitz.
XXXXVI. Pz.-Korps: Senslau (11 km nordwestlich Dirschau)
7.)Gebührt Fernschreiben
8.) 2. Armee: 1 Feindpanzer bewegungsunfähig geschossen, 2 M.Pi., 2 Pz.-Büchsen, 2 s.M.G., 1 Pak vernichtet, 18 Scharfschützenabschüsse, 1 s.M.G. erbeutet.

Von Division Berlin wurden in den Kämpfen bei Sydowswiese und Sophiental in der Zeit vom 20.-23.2. vernichtet bezw. er-
- 6-

Parts of the Army Group Vistula daily report (*Tagesmeldung*) of 24 February 1945, with information about the *Charlemagne* Division's activities near Czarne (Hammerstein). (United States National Archives)

The *Charlemagne* was made ready for combat on 24 February at 1000 hours, with units departing for their start positions three hours later. Long after the end of the war, the atmosphere prevailing at that time among the formations was characterized by former *Waffen-Rottenführer* Robert Soulat in the following words:

> It is bloody cold and snowing. Snowflakes endlessly whirl in the air in the lemon streaks of headlights … At dawn we move wrapped around the ears in all available blankets and rags. We are not particularly talked about when we walk like ghosts under an overwhelming gray sky across these sad plains covered with snow, crossed by forests and lakes; we are supposed to defend it![25]

The first contact with the enemy was made by soldiers of the 2nd battalion of the *57. Grenadier Regiment der SS*. With Barkowo taken by the Soviets, a stop was ordered in Bińcze (Bärenwalde). At about 1500 hours, there was a fire exchange between the reconnaissance platoon led by *Waffen-Untersturmführer* Erdozain, and – curiously – Russians from Barkowo dressed in German uniforms. After several hours of hard fighting, the town was recaptured, but the battalion came under fire from a nearby forest and the unit lost 12 men. *Waffen-Hauptsturmführer* Obitz arranged his forces as follows: the 5th Company was placed in the centre, about 5km southeast of the village. On the southern edge of Barkowo were troops of the 6th Company, while the 8th Company, armed with heavy machine guns, manned posts on the road leading to Bińcze, today's Voivodship Road 201.[26]

At the same time, units under *Waffen-Obersturmführer* Fenet were operating in the Uniechów area. Positions taken by them were shelled by Soviet mortars, but the Frenchmen hit back strongly,quickly using almost all of their 81mm ammunition. There were several soldiers killed, while among the injured was the commander of one of the teams, *Waffen-Sturmmann* Yvon Trémel, whose hands were struck

the Third Reich, in the form of a chevron. During the fighting in Pomerania, two types of shield patches were used: veterans of the LVF most often used the early pattern intended for this unit, where the upper edge had an embroidered inscription of 'France'; the others had the pattern introduced in the second half 1943 for soldiers fighting in the ranks of the *Waffen-SS* (characterized by the lack of inscriptions and a thick, black border). As veterans recall, both insignia designs were very rarely placed on coats. In addition, some soldiers adhering to the ideas of monarchist France, including *Waffen-Oberführer* Edgar Puaud, deliberately did not sew divisional insignia on uniforms, explaining that the proper colours for their homeland were white and gold, i.e. the symbols of the Bourbon dynasty. A separate issue is the black cuff bands with the embroidered name *Charlemagne*, which were to appear during the fighting in Pomerania only in the case of a group of artillerymen from the Protectorate of Bohemia and Moravia. The removal of this insignia was ordered by *SS-Brigadeführer* Gustav Krukenberg, claiming that only soldiers who had fought in the battle had the right to wear it.

25   Memories of *Waffen-Rottenführer* Robert Soulat preserved in the author's archive, p. 1.
26   R. Forbes, *For Europe…*, pp. 253–54.

Bińcze (Barenwalde) Distillery in February 2017. It was here on 24 February 1945 that 2nd battalion of *57. Grenadier-Regiment der SS* of the *Charlemagne* Division took up defensive positions. (Author: Łukasz Gładysiak)

The Voivodship Road 201 from Barkowo (Barkenfelde) to Bińcze (Bärenwalde) in March 2017. There were defensive positions there of the 3rd Company of the *58. Grenadier Regiment der SS*, acompanied by Latvians from the *15. SS-Grenadier Division*, on 25 February 1945. (Photo: Łukasz Gładysiak)

South of Barkowo in March 2017, where there were defensive positions of the 6th Company of the *57. Grenadier Regiment der SS* on 24 February 1945. (Author: Łukasz Gładysiak)

by shrapnel (he managed to evacuate himself to the dressing station). There was a constant exchange of fire with the Soviets facing them, creating a chaotic situation. However, the main reason for the confusion was the lack of communication between the sub-units, and there were cases of shelling their own positions. Red Army troops, regardless of the hastily built   machine-gun positions of their opponents, rushed forward in waves, reminiscent of scenes from the trench warfare of the First World War. The sight of entire Russian sections falling under gunfire was hard to bear for many in the *Charlemagne*, especially those who had not served on the front lines before. Despite this, the Frenchmen managed to achieve some short-term successes. Rushing northeast from the estate of Gut Schönwerder, after covering less than 3km, some of Fenet's men briefly entered Uniechów. Soldiers of the 3rd Company, led by *Waffen-Untersturmführer* Counil, were the first to reach the town.[27] However, Counil was killed there, having been hit by mortar fire, and he was replaced by *Waffen-Oberscharführer* Quicampoix. The French grenadiers gained control of a junction next to the village church (the modern Church of St Bartholomew the Apostle). The attack was carried out by four independent grenadier groups and was focused on farms located in the northern part of the village. A cemetery was another goal, which was targetted by the 2nd Company under *Waffen-Obersturmführer* Ivan Bartolomei.

27   *Waffen-Grenadier-Division der…*, p. 11.

A picture taken in March 2017 of the crossroads near the church of Uniechów (Heinrichswalde), which was the target of a counterattack by the 3rd Company of the *57. Waffen-Grenadier Regiment der SS* on 24 February 1945. (Author: Łukasz Gładysiak)

The road leading to the lake of Uniechów (Heinrichswalde) in March 2017, one of the attacking routes taken by the *57. Waffen-Grenadier Regiment der SS* on 24 February 1945. (Author: Łukasz Gładysiak)

Soldiers approaching the cemetery came under fire from automatic weapons. The commander of one of the platoons who had previously served in the French Navy, *Waffen-Unterscharführer* Mauclair, suffered fatal wounds. A moment later, another NCO, former Vichy militiaman *Waffen-Oberscharführer* Gastinel, was killed, struck by a bullet as he tried to deliver a report to the company commander. The cemetery in Uniechów was also targeted by Soviet artillery, as a result of which most of *Waffen-Unterscharführer* Franchart's platoon were eliminated. Being cut off from the rest of the battalion, Bartolomei decided to retreat on his own.

Finally, after several attempts by the Soviets to recapture the town, it was decided to retreat, leaving at least a dozen fallen comrades on the battlefield, including the aforementioned commander of the 3rd Company (it cannot be ruled out that his body was moved to the property of Gut Schönwerder, where due to the pace of the retreat, it was not able to be buried[28]). On 25 February, around 0300 hours, the group set up defensive positions around the shore of Lake Wieldządz, about halfway between Barkowo and Bińcze. This proved a smart move, as soon afterwards, Uniechów and the surrounding area was again captured by the Soviets. In addition, Fenet had failed to establish the hoped-for contact with any elements of the Latvian *15. SS- Grenadier Division*. In this situation, any lengthening of the defensive line was not justified.

During these engagements fought by the 1st battalion of the *57. Waffen-Grenadier Regiment der SS*, it is worth mentioning how the officers tried to remedy shortages of field radio, so as not to interrupt communications between sub-units. As in the war of 1914–18 and earlier conflicts, horses were used, being taken from the farms where they remained despite the progress of the Red Army. One of those who rode with messages for *Waffen-Hauptsturmführer* de Bourmont's staff was the adjutant, *Waffen-Obersturmführer* de Londaiz.

Before dawn, Fenet's men clashed with the Soviet infantry again. Fearing encirclement, it was decided to relocate to Bińcze to join forces with the staff of the 1st battalion. Bartolomei, whose 2nd Company was still fighting in isolation, was still missing, but it was not known at the time that his troops were heading back to Czarne.

On the morning of 25 February, Bińcze also became the target of the displaced 2nd battalion of the *57. Waffen-Grenadier Regiment der SS*. After creating well-camouflaged positions, the French awaited the arrival of the enemy. They first appeared opposite the 6th Company but were forced to retreat after fire conducted from a distance of only 20 metres. During this skirmish, the first prisoners were captured, with three Russians sent to the rear for questioning. Reconnaissance by Soviet units led to the area coming under artillery fire, including Katyusha rocket launchers. After an hour's onslaught, Soviet infantry resumed the attack. Facing superior Soviet forces, and with

---

28   Information about leaving the bodies of 10 comrades was confirmed in the 1990s by *Waffen-Hauptscharführer* Bucoiran, an NCO of the 1st battalion of the *57. Waffen-Grenadier Regiment der SS*.

his own casualties mounting, *Waffen-Haupsturmführer* Obitz decided to retreat. In the confusion, some platoons took the wrong road, often moving into enemy positions. A participant in these events, Maurice Comte from the 57th's 5th Company, later recalled:

> We advanced blindly, equipped only with light weapons and one, maybe two machine guns. Initially, being under the cover of the forest, we managed to avoid contact with the Russians. Soon after that, before our eyes an enemy column rose from the ground. The T-34 was in front, followed by a Stalin tank [probably an IS-2] and another T-34. The infantry accompanying the vehicles did not seem to notice us. Gun barrels were directed towards the ground all the time. Suddenly shrapnel began to ripple around me. Next to me, our unit's commander, *Waffen-Obersturmführer* Artus, fell to the ground with a fatal wound in his neck. I heard behind me: 'The lieutenant is dead!' All we [could] do [was] escape.[29]

An equally difficult situation developed in the section manned by the 2nd battalion of the *58. Waffen-Grenadier Regiment der SS*, which was located in the area of Biernatka (Bärenhütte). There, again and again, gunshots, mortars and rocket launchers were fired into the French positions. The Russians infantry attacked in constant waves. In a short time, individual companies lost contact with each other, which required the running of dispatch riders. A few hours later, in the section manned by the 3rd Company under the command of *Waffen-Untersturmführer* Yves Rigeade, the most seriously wounded comrades from the regiment began to appear. To everyone's surprise, Latvians from the *15. SS-Grenadier Division* also appeared.

Employing the remaining mortar ammunition, it was decided to protect the road to the town from Bińcze. In this episode, the infantry company recently launched into the fight was commanded by *Waffen-Obersturmführer* Français. The loss of horses due to the shelling of the enemy meant that the gunners did not receive ammunition. In order not to delay the planned retreat, all the guns were blown up using hand grenades. A scouting party directed towards Bińcze, which had the opportunity to wedge into the enemy's position and then move back towards Czarne, retreated back at the sight of enemy tanks entering the village.

Shortly afterwards, the 3rd Company was cut off from the rest of the battalion. On 25 February, around 1000 hours, a Soviet armoured unit with infantry and flame-throwing tanks appeared opposite its outposts. Deprived of *Panzerfaust* grenades, the French opened fire, focusing on the Soviet infantry. The commander of one of the platoons, *Waffen-Oberscharführer* Blonet, in an almost suicidal move, attacked a T-34 armed with a only hand grenade, but it had no effect. The tanks kept on coming, their caterpillar tracks crushing the wounded lying in the field.

---

29   R. Forbes, *For Europe…*, pp. 256–59.

Just as *Waffen-Untersturmführer* Rigeade feared the end was coming for his men, the Russians pulled back. The reason was an unexpected attack by the 57th's 1st Battalion breaking through to Bińcze. These troops brought with them *Panzerfaust* grenade launchers,which quickly destroyed two Soviet tanks emerging from a nearby forest. Despite their efforts, the unit retreated towards the railway line connecting Bińcze with Czarn. Confusion, which became the hallmark of the French division's combat debut, meant that contact with Blonet's platoon was lost. After wandering around the area for some time, Blonct's men eventually managed to get to Szczecinek.[30] Other troops were then assigned to the 1st battalion.

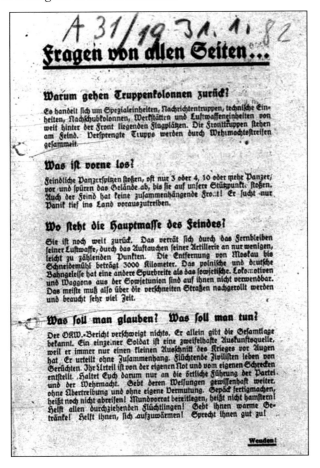

The *Die Panzerfaust* front newspaper issued at the end of February 1945 with a description of *Wehrmacht* conditions of that time. Similar papers were surely sent to the French SS soldiers in Pomerania. (United States National Archives)

30   Ibid., pp. 264–66.

On the afternoon of 25 February, Bińcze finally fell to the Red Army, which then began an attack towards Czarne from the Uniechów area. The air was swarming with aviation with red stars on their wings. *Waffen-Obersturmführer* Fenet decided to retreat towards Czarne, using, whenever possible, forest cover. Moving via Biernatka, a battalion subordinate to Fenet, or rather a battalion battle group, reached the village of Nadziejewo [Hansfelde], located on the eastern approach to Czarne. In the nearby fir forest, they fought with a Soviet reconnaissance platoon. After exiting the main road (today's Voivodship Road 201), the French encountered a crowd of civilians fleeing from the Russians. Around 2100 hours, exhausted soldiers crossed the gates of the camp from which they set out to fight the previous day. There they found comrades from a battle group which had assaulted Uniechów, with some of the weapons from the 2nd company, whose combat capability at that time did not go beyond a single platoon.

Even before Fenet's unit reached Czarne, the area became the centre of events for the *Charlemagne* Division. In addition to decimated sub-units that had moved in after the previous day's fight, a company of sappers and the 110-strong 10th (anti-tank) company of the regiment checked in. Before they could take any action, they were forced to abandon three artillery pieces that lacked ammunition, tractors and horses. The group took over posts north of the railway line, facing their weapons east. Around noon, the first contact was made with the enemy, who directed mortar fire on the French positions. This did not, however, prevent the preparation within a few hours of a strongpoint reinforced with two heavy 150mm infantry guns and six 75mm guns. Some of this equipment probably came from transport previously taken at the Hessian railway station in Jossa, originally intended for the *28. SS-Division 'Wallonien'*. The division also received mortars from the 8th Company of the 57th Regiment under the command of *Waffen-Unterscharführer* Terret and a group of *SS-Panzerjäger Abteilung 33* soldiers under the command of *Waffen-Oberjunker* Radici. Historian Robert Forbes also mentions the deployment of several 88mm guns on approaches to towns from the east. The regiment's staff was moved to a field post near the railway tracks. In the same area, there was probably also a first aid station run by Dr Métais. *Waffen-Untersturmführer* Christian Martret was responsible for communication between the individual sub-units. The *Charlemagne* Division's headquarters were located in Olszanów (Elsenau) several kilometres east, regardless of the risk of being cut off there.

Soviet aircraft were the first to hit the French positions in Czarne. Veterans recalled that the planes flew so low that sometimes they could see the heads of the pilots sitting in the cabins. Then, in the early afternoon, about 20 Soviet tanks started to advance. Two of them fell prey to anti-tank guns. Another, having broken off its caterpillar track, rolled off the embankment and came to a halt. Two tanks struck mines laid by divisional sappers and were hit by *Panzerfaust* grenades fired by *Waffen-Oberscharführer* Barclay.

Enemy fire concentrated on those positions where there was no ammunition. Among the seriously wounded were the commander of the 10th (anti-tank) Company of the *58. Regiment*, *Waffen-Obersturmführer* Serge Krotoff, and his deputy, *Waffen-Oberjunker* Vincenot. Seeing the lack of reaction from some of the artillerymen, Soviet tanks began to target their positions. Infantry followed behind the tanks. With the Russians enjoying an advantage of ten to one in troops, some members of the *Charlemagne* staff were also thrown into the battle. Even *SS-Standartenführer* Zimmermann and *Waffen-Oberführer* Puaud joined the front line, firing submachine guns. Around 1500 hours, the French line began to crack. There was a desperate shortage of ammunition, for both artillery and small arms. Half an hour later, the first sub-units began to retreat, heading towards the railway station, which was already besieged by the enemy. Before long the station was abandoned, the men retreating to the vicinity of the POW camp on the section manned by the remains of the 1st and 2nd companies of the regiment, but not before they managed to destroy another two Soviet tanks with *Panzerfausts*.

Clearly unable to defend Czarne any period, the commander of the *XVIII Gebirgskorps*, *General der Infanterie* Hochbaum, agreed to withdraw the French division to the vicinity of Olszanów, ordering its headquarters to move to Koczała (Flötenstein), where he also placed the corps command. The implementation of both these tasks was made more difficult because the units, tired from lengthy fighting, had to move almost parallel to the axis of the Soviet attack.

Koczała (Flötenstein) in March 2017. In the second half of February 1945, this was the location of the German *XVIII Gebirgskorps* headquarters, as well as of the *Charlemagne Division* command. (Author: Łukasz Gładysiak)

A rather unbelievable story is said to have happened at this time, which is quoted by the author of the French-language monograph *33. Waffen-Grenadier Division der SS*, Jean Mabire. According to his findings, *SS-Standartenführer* Zimmermann was summoned to the headquarters of the *XVIII Gebirgskorps* located in a manor house in Rzeczenica, along with several officers not mentioned by name who were part of the German inspection team accompanying the staff of the *Charlemagne*. After the meeting, everyone, including *General* Hochbaum, left the building. Suddenly, from a distance, they saw a Soviet T-34 tank rushing straight at them. A shell fired from its 85mm gun hit a car parked in front of the house. A moment later, a *Panzerfaust* grenade was fired towards the attackers, launched by an unknown lieutenant, and the Russians fled.[31]

Zimmermann remained with the staff of the *XVIII Gebirgskorps*, which made it impossible for him to send orders for the *Charlemagne Division* command to move to its new location. At that time, during the night of 25–26 February, the Frenchmen retreated towards Olszanów, and new defensive positions were organized. Two platoons set off first, having not yet participated in the fighting of the staff company (also called known as the *Compagnie d'Honneur*, or Company of Honour). The group, armed with *Panzerfausts*, was commanded by *SS-Obersturmführer* Wilhelm Weber, who did not speak French. Marching to their designated positions, his men passed a slowly moving column of soldiers and civilians, in which the terrified inhabitants of the surrounding towns were mixed up with members of the broken Latvian sub-units, which included, to the amazement of the Frenchmen, a large group of seriously injured comrades from the *57. Regiment*.[32]

Weber's men took up positions in the forest, a few hundred metres from the western edge of one of the exit roads from Olszanów. In the early afternoon of 26 February, they destroyed a T-34, which came from the vicinity of Biernatka. A second tank was soon also hit, its crew being killed by small-arms fire while trying to repair a broken caterpillar. Members of the platoon who had been kept in reserve until first contact with the enemy were less lucky. As recalled after the end of the war by the head of one of the teams, *Waffen-Unterführeranwärter* Louis Levast, on the way to their positions, the group was shelled with 85mm shells from a distance of less than a kilometre. Most of the men were wounded, with many killed, so they were unable to provide proper support for the Honour Company.

To challenge by combat the numerical superiority of the attacking Soviet forces, the soldiers began to install anti-tank traps along the road. These were primarily *Panzerfaust* grenade launchers tied to trees and aimed at the road. They would be fired after a wire spun across the road was broken. Shortly thereafter, the French Grenadiers hidden in the bushes and between the buildings heard explosions, followed by a series of machine-gun bursts. From a group of about a dozen tanks

31   J. Mabire, *La Division…*, p. 353.
32   R. Forbes, *For Europe…*, p. 276.

that advanced on Olszanów, only three managed to pass through the traps. One of these was immediately hit by another *Panzerfaust*. The next one was immobilized by a grenade thrown by *SS-Obersturmführer* Weber. When he was aiming at the last of the tanks, Soviet infantry rushed forward to help the crews. The first wave of attack collapsed under small-arms fire from the French. It was a similar story with the second assault. Expecting further attacks, the staff company began a controlled retreat towards the cemetery. The wounded were also moved there (later, unable to be evacuated, they were murdered by the Russians). Around 1730 hours, the Honour Company took its final position of the battle. The companies of both Grenadier divisions, which were almost on the verge of disintegration, came to their aid, having fought almost uninterrupted for two days. Although the sight of 19 destroyed Soviet tanks encouraged the Frenchmen, it was rightly expected that the Russians had dozens more in reserve, along with an overwhelming number of infantry. The fighting, often hand-to-hand, continued until late evening.

Olszanów (Elsenau) crossroads in March 2017, where in February 1945 the French *SS Compagnie d'Honneur* led by *SS-Obersturmführer* Wilhelm Weber hunted Soviet tanks. (Author: Łukasz Gładysiak)

Having no more grenades or *Panzerfausts*, and thus unable to offer further resistance, the staff company, whose strength had decreased by more than half, fled Olszanów.[33] The French soldiers were now led by the 58th Regiment's 1st Company commander, *Waffen-Obersturmführer* Fantin, who initially intended to return to Czarne. However, having heard of Soviet progress, he divided his group into three platoons under the command of *Waffen-Oberjunker* de Brangelin, *Waffen-Oberjunker* Lapart and *Waffen-Oberscharführer* Bonnafouse and decided to break through to the north and avoid further fighting. He believed that it would be possible to make contact with larger German units there and thus save the lives of his men.

Part of the German Army Group Vistula daily report of 25 February 1945 with a list of German units deployed in Pomerania. The *Charlemagne* Division is mentioned, with the note that it then had only nine platoons available. (United States National Archives)

33   J. Trigg, *Hitler's Gauls…*, pp. 91–92.

Sometime earlier, *SS-Brigadeführer* Krukenberg's staff and the communications company were evacuated from the area, leaving behind all their radio equipment. The division's staff managed to get to Koczała the same day, meeting *SS-Standartenführer* Zimmermann, and the unit then moved west, straight into the hands of the enemy. Surrounded by Soviet tanks, they were unable to resist. They were almost completely eliminated. Only a few, maybe a dozen or so soldiers, managed to reach Czarne and continue their retreat.[34]

The school at Olszanów (Elsenau) in March 2017, the possible location of the *Charlemagne* Division's headquarters on 26 February 1945. There was also a field medic post there. (Photo Łukasz Gładysiak)

The last centre of resistance in the Czarne area was the village of Biernatka, defended by the survivors of the 1st battalion of the *58. Waffen-Grenadier Regiment der SS*, reinforced by the remains of several companies of its sister regiment, including a few mortars and infantry guns. The Russians then began shelling the town. Soviet snipers also appeared, hunting for French officers. By 2000 hours, *Waffen-Sturmbannführer* Raybaud had run out of larger-calibre ammunition. Due to the real risk of being cut off, the soldiers began to retreat. To slow down the pursuit, they left a large supply of alcohol from abandoned farms in Biernatka, hoping that the Soviets would be

34   R. Forbes, *For Europe...*, p. 286.

distracted by it.[35] Among the dozens who remained and died in the village was the adjutant of the staff of the *57. Regiment*, *Waffen-Obersturmführer* Jean Artus, who was killed while attempting to destroy a Soviet tank with a *Panzerfaust*.

The evacuation towards Szczecinek continued, with Czarne finally falling into the hands of the Red Army on 28 February. Three days earlier, before the defence of the town began, the motor column and supply sub-division of the *33. Waffen-Grenadier-Division der SS Charlemagne* had left. Whilst the combat positions were beingoccupied in the area of the railway line, it was time for the rear units to flee. This group, numbering about 120 troops who did not usually take part in front-line fighting – which was sometimes called the Alarm Company – was led by *SS-Sturmbannführer* Katzian. It was divided into three platoons. The first, the best prepared for action with hand weapons and a 7.92mm *MG 34* machine gun, were German inspection officers of the division staff. The second platoon included writers, secretaries, translators, tailors, and authorizing officers, and had several machine guns, a 7.92mm *Mauser wz. 1898k* and several pistols and grenades. The third platoon, which acted as a rearguard, was a group gathered around *Waffen-Obersturmführer* Darrigade. A member of the second platoon of the Alarm Company, *Waffen-Rottenführer* Soulat, recalled:

> The camp looks like an anthill, people are running everywhere. Motorcyclists, liaison on horses and in passenger cars appear and disappear. We manage to spend part of the night in a barrack with broken glass, on a pile of straw with a doubtful smell, probably stuffed with some bugs … Here in Hammerstein it is difficult to have a fairly clear picture of the battle that began at night. Only salvos from *Stalinorgeln* [the famous Soviet *Katyusha* truck-mounted rocket launchers) whose characteristic sound comes to us from time to time remind [us] that just a few kilometres from here our soldiers are fighting furiously and…. dying … It seems that the situation is serious. The survivors from the 57th Regiment reach the camp. Their eyes are burning, their hands are shaking … These comrades are mostly completely demoralized by the numerical superiority of the enemy. Pessimism reaches its zenith.[36]

The Alarm Company set off on 26 February at 0500 hours, probably burning most divisional documents beforehand.[37] Using hastily repaired trucks, they managed to reach Szczecinek without losses, although some of the vehicles failed along the way, as Soulat continued:

---

35   The record of this event was contained in anonymous recollections forwarded to the author on 1 September 2012 by Stanisław Kłoskowski from Olszanów.
36   *Waffen-Rottenführer* Robert Soulat testimony…, p. 3.
37   The qutoed NCO recalled: "I soon [reach] a barrack in which, in a 'goat' stove, I burn all my personal papers and photos, except for the military booklet."

The engine of our truck starts to snort and finally [packs up]: we are forced to continue walking. I begin to curse our damned bad luck. Fortunately, the condition of the road is amazingly good. We go by the side of the road on both sides. Latvian carts are retreating in the opposite direction. In the distance, on our right, the glow of burning villages ominously illuminates the horizon. After passing six, maybe seven kilometres, we reach the intersection, on which stands a gendarme from our division. Seeing us like a possessed man, he waves his arms, ordering [us] to hide in a roadside ditch. Apparently, the area where we found ourselves is already 'cleaned' by enemy machine guns. After a brief consultation with an officer ... Katzian decides to lead our platoon along a beaten path to the left of the main road. We walk half a kilometre, then another two hundred metres across the field, to the edge of the forest. We take positions in the wilderness. The first platoon is falling [behind] about eight hundred metres to our left. There is only a void between us ... The trees and the ground are covered with snow, which has been heavy in previous days. Now the temperature is above zero, everything is melting. There is no chance to lie down on the ground without the risk of getting completely wet ... We can manage something there, but first you have to get out of this damned encirclement! We walk quite chaotically along the forest edge. Fortunately, moss and needles suppress our steps. Together with three colleagues I am moving in the advance guard. I realize that if we meet the enemy, I will probably be the first to be hit, knowing life, right in the guts. To my surprise, I accept this 'verdict' with complete calmness, as if I subconsciously felt that breaking [out] from Hammerstein would really succeed ... *Waffen-Sturmbannführer* Katzian is right behind us, with a submachine gun on his chest. Arm-in-arm with him walks a friend of [the] *Waffen-Rottenführer* with a machine gun at his hip. At the edge of the forest, the officer stops the group and orders a 'masked stop'. On the road we are marching, something is starting to happen; you can see the silhouettes of soldiers that are difficult to recognize. I bring the cartridge into the chamber of my rifle. It turns out after a while that they are French who, like us, are trying to escape the expected Soviet fire at all costs. There is not a minute to lose. You have to move on ... I am totally exhausted, I can barely walk. Although I try to move as quickly as possible, I feel like I'm growing into Pomeranian soil and literally standing still. It seems to me that I look like a puppet whose strings have been cut. After a night spent practically standing in melting snow, crossing a stream with water reaching to the knees and almost sprinting running on the moss, I feel dead.[38]

At the same time, a struggle for survival in the face of the enemy's armoured attacks was fought by elements of the 7th Company of the *58. Regiment*, which was near

38 Ibid., pp. 5-6, 8-9.

Krępsk (Krapsk), a few kilometres northeast of Olszanów. Its troops became the target of massive attacks by Soviet armoured vehicles. A description of the elimination of one of the units is contained in materials provided to the author on 1 September 2012 by Stanisław Kłoskowski from Olszanów, whose family had been researching the history of the Szczecinek region for several decades, from one of the participants in the event, Alain Boutier:

> It is February 25, 1945, 6.00 PM. My team was sent to the area of the transition between the Olszanowskie and Gwieździńskie lakes, [and] in the evening we took a position at the edge of the forest. We listened to the approaching tanks. Waiting for the order to retreat from the company staff, we were surprised that such was not coming. We decided to make contact with him ourselves, but it turned out that it was too late. We have been encircled from all sides. The first Soviets approached from Krępsk; our position was about a hundred metres from the road leading to this town. Suddenly the exchange of fire began. Young pines gave no cover. We had to lie on the snow, [and] branches cut off with bullets fell on us. A few fell. My friend Hamelin was hit in the back of the helmet and fell on the spot. Seriously wounded, they died in torment. We saw Russians running with shouts of 'Urra' and 'For Stalin'. They crossed the nearby ravines; the end was approaching. I decided to leave my current position. I noticed my next friend – Lauglanet, who was leaning against a tree and protected the retreat with rifle fire. After a while he was hit, I saw him fall to the ground. The fight ceased. I was wondering what to do. I escaped towards the lake and headed along the shore, wading in the water. I saw an enemy unit walking down the valley, as if standing in a dead end. I changed the direction, tried to escape from the nearby gorge with the rest of my strength. I heard shots from every side. Finally, I found myself on a plain, [where] not far, about three hundred metres away from me was a slope descending into the water. Bullets tore open the snowy ground. I threw myself [down] and lay flat for a moment. Staying in this position for about fifteen minutes, I came to the conclusion that the shooting had ceased. Frozen, I started to run; with fast jumps I moved away from the previous place and thus slipped away from the opponent.

There were only two soldiers from Alain Boutier's team who survived the clash. The others, probably 200, were buried in a mass grave near Krępsk, somewhere between the two lakes.[39]

At the same time, the exodus of the 1st Company of the *58. Regiment* under the command of *Waffen-Obersturmführer* Fantin, which was to join the division only in April 1945, was ongoing. The company's core was formed of experienced LVF veterans. On 27 February, they arrived in the vicinity of Koczała (the same place

39   Alain Boutier testimony preserved in author's archive.

Krępsk (Krapsk) in March 2017, an area where the major part of the 7th Company of the *58. Waffen-Grenadier Regiment der SS* was destroyed on 26 February 1945. (Photo Łukasz Gładysiak)

where, on 2 March, another French group appeared – 100 soldiers gathered by *SS-Obersturmführer* Weber, former commander of the tank hunter unit from Biernatka, which in connection with the result of the fight against Soviet armoured forces gained the nickname 'Cyclone'). The next day, *Waffen-Oberscharführer* Gagnerone's platoon set off towards the village of Miłocice (Falkenhagen), where on 1 March he made contact with the crews of eight unidentified self-propelled guns, most likely belonging to *Schwere Panzerjäger Abteilung 743*. Under the cover of darkness, the vehicles joined a French assault against Miastko. In the morning, the unit was supported by a local garrison, which was desperately resisting the Soviet 10th Guards Infantry Division. That same day, in view of the overwhelming advantage of the enemy, a decision was made to head to the Trzebiatkowa (Radensfeld) railway station, where on the night of 2–3 March, the platoon encountered a group of 24 French prisoners of war from the 1940 campaign. Attempts were made to dissuade their companions from their plan to reach the town of Miastko, already occupied in large part by the Red Army, but ultimately it failed. The next day, the Franco-German units again attempted to attack the town. Despite the desperate resistance of the Soviets, the attack was successful. If you believe the accounts of participants in these events, among the civilians murdered in retaliation for the occupation of USSR territories by the Third Reich, the above-mentioned former prisoners were also found.[40]

On 4 March, Gagnerone's platoon made its way to Sławno (Schlawe), where it came across 300 comrades who had not managed to reach Czarne. This unit was headed by *Waffen-Hauptsturmführer* René André Obitz, who it seems had broken through from Barkowo on his own. That same day, he took command of the entire French forces in the city, thereby creating an improvised marching battalion operating for the next month regardless of the *Charlemagne* Division. This unit, at its peak, including a group of artillerymen delegated to Pomerania from the training ground in the Protectorate of Bohemia and Moravia, numbered up to 600 troops. On 5 March, after an enforced stop caused by the lack of a locomotive able to pull the unit towards Wejherowo, the group finally managed to reach Słupsk (Stolp), where their transport was attacked by Soviet planes. As a result of the bombing, eight soldiers of the battalion were killed, and its commander, as well as 60 other Frenchmen, were wounded. Eventually, the train managed to reach Wejherowo, and the unit was most likely located near Bolszewo. Before joining the fight for the so-called 'Tri-City' – Gdańsk (Danzig), Gdynia (Gotenhafen) and Sopot (Zoppot) – the marching battalion was joined by one more group, which had broke through from the Baltic Sea, some 20 Frenchmen who had previously served in the 1st Company of the *58. Regiment*. Over the next three weeks, divided into three company battlegroups led by *Waffen-Oberscharführer* Bonnafous, *Waffen-Oberjunker* Lapart and *Waffen-Oberjunker* Chatrousse, they fought together for Gdańsk and Gdynia. Finally, on 1 April, some 100 survivors of *Waffen-Hauptsturmführer* Obitz's force were evacuated to Denmark, from where they were transported to the vicinity of Carpin in Mecklenburg.

The numbers taking part in the combat debut of the *33. Waffen-Grenadier Division der SS Charlemagne* in the Czarne area has caused researchers great problems almost since the end of the war. The number of and irregular arrival at transport sites, the lack of communication between the sub-units and the chaos this caused, as well as the merger and division of companies and platoons, made it difficult to clearly identify French losses. The only value that currently seems certain is that some 4,500 soldiers eventually took part in the Pomeranian battles described so far. The smallest number of dead that can be found in the literature on the subject is 500, including five officers, according to Jean Mabire and Richard Landwehr, among others. Christian La Mazière indicates the number was twice as high, although in this case those who were listed as missing are also included. The author also encountered a statement about 3,000 having fallen, although this figure seems far from reality.

---

40   It is worth noting that this was not the only German counterattack carried out on this part of the Pomeranian front at this time. On 1 March 1, the *4. SS-Polizei Division* joined an attack on elements of the Soviet 3rd Guards Tank Corps stationed in Miastko and its immediate vicinity. Its soldiers managed to eject the leading elements of the 19th Guards Tank Brigade from around Sępolno Wielkie (Gross Karzenburg) and regain control over the fortifications of the *Pommernstellung* line at Lake Bobięcińskie Wielkie for a short time.

At the start of the struggle of the group formed around the 1st Company of the *58. Waffen-Grenadier Regiment der SS* on the eastern border of the Pomeranian Province, the main part of the *33. Waffen-Grenadier-Division der SS Charlemagne* was moved on 27 February 1945 from the area of Czarne to Szczecinek. The vanguard, which first entered this city, was made up of the soldiers of the staff of the 2nd Battalion and the 5th Company of the *58. Regiment*, but among them were some additions. The military secured quarters that the local *Wehrmacht* command had designated in the barracks located at today's ul. Słowiańska. There, they encountered sub-units in the area of Czarne, at the same time learning about the hopeless situation in which the group found itself in this area. As *Waffen-Rottenführer* Soulat, quoted several times, recalled, the atmosphere in the city contrasted vividly with the feelings engendered by exhausting fights and the evacuation of the French:

> We are walking busy streets. It seems that the inhabitants are not even aware of the close presence of Russians. Everyone maintains the appearance of normality, calmness and completely unreasonable, given the state of preparation of Neustettin for defence, security. Even the appearance of muddy, unshaven and completely broken soldiers of our division is not able to bring them to the ground or give a taste of what awaits them inevitably within a dozen or so hours. Some very bourgeois-looking passerby whom we stopped, explaining briefly the situation on the first line, does not believe his own ears. His eyes widen like saucers, probably treating us [as] crazy.[41]

That afternoon, a train arrived from Fulda transporting eight 150mm heavy field guns (or maybe 105mm light field howitzers) from the Czechoslovakia, which were directed to Pomerania, along with nine 37mm anti-aircraft guns and 150 soldiers under *Waffen-Hauptsturmführer* Jean Basompierre. The commander was ordered to remain in Wildflecken, but wanting to immediately join their companions fighting in the front line, he refused to comply with this order. All forces were told to prepare for combat as ordinary infantry.[42] After a short time, the area was targeted by a Soviet aircraft attack. Fortunately for the French, the transport survived the shelling, and one of the crews of a 3.7cm *Flugbawehrkanone* even managed to seriously damage an enemy machine. In view of the risk of further raids, it was decided that the artillery would be moved, most likely towards Kołobrzeg (Kolberg), considered at that time relatively safe, and above all well prepared for defence. Neither did the division staff intend to stay in the city on the Trzesiecko Lake for too long. On 27 February, it was decided to march towards the Baltic Sea. Białogard (Belgard an der Persante) was to be the new assembly point, with 0700 hours the next day designated as the departure hour.

---

41   *Waffen-Rottenführer* Robert Soulat testimony..., p. 11.
42   Letters of Robert Soulat to author, sent on 3 and 12 August 2011.

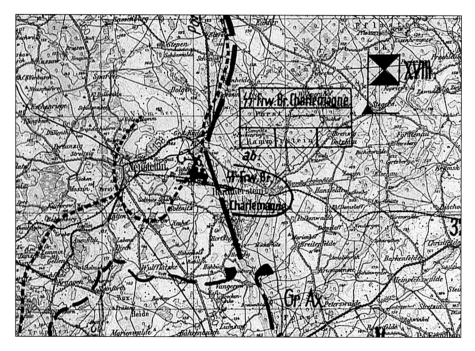

Part of a *Heeresgruppe Weichsel* map with German positions on 27 February 1945. There is a *33. Waffen-Grenadier Division der SS Charlemagne* emplacement in the Szczecinek (Neustettin) area. (United States National Archives)

An hour after midnight on 28 February, at Szczecin station, the loading of heavily damaged assets of the *33. Waffen-Grenadier-Division der SS* onto wagons began. A moment later, an anti-tank alarm was announced in the city.[43] Panic broke out in the French ranks, which were now essentially deprived of any means to stop Soviet tanks. Many sleeping soldiers had not bdeen informed about the move order. Such a fate befell a soldier by the name of Marotin, who, awakened by an artillery cannonade, failed to find his compatriots. Wandering around the city, he was detained by a *Wehrmacht* officer and assigned to a hastily created alarm unit, numbering about 50 men, supported by four anti-tank guns. He took part in a skirmish, during which he managed to eliminate two Soviet tanks. However, the enemy's retreat did not last long. After a few minutes, the Russians returned with more tanks. Marotin recalled after the war: "A big guy in a mustard uniform threw grenades [at us] ... I fell to the ground with my mouth and eyes full of earth, I was stunned. A German grenadier to my right mowed [down] the Soviet giant with a precise [volley]."

43   J. Miniewicz, B. Perzyk, *Wał Pomorski...*, p. 99.

Soviet artillery thundered, preparing the way for the final assault. Due to the risk of the line being broken by the leading Red Army units, which were close to blocking the railway lines from the city – at that time the Soviet cavalry was also starting to attack from Lake Trzesiecko – the soldiers decided to walk on foot to Połczyn Zdrój (Bad Polzin), more than 40km to the east. An alternative retreat route appeared then through Bobolice (Bublitz) and Koszalin (Köslin), which probably largely coincided with the course of today's National Road 11. Wagons with equipment had already been loaded at the initiative of *Waffen–Untersturmführer* Raymond (Robert?) Daffas.[44] They were to move northwards with the *Panzerzug 72* armoured train.[45] During the hooking up of wagons, there were close-range fire fights with the Russians. However, the train departed and later reached Kołobrzeg, where one of its components – *Panzerzug 72A* under the command of HauptmannCaptain Gerhard Röming – took part in the battles to defend the fortress.[46]

Many soldiers of the *Charlemagne* Division, recalling the experience of the evacuation from Czarne, tried to independently organize a move to the next location that was free from enemy forces. *Waffen–Rottenführer* Soulat stated long after the war:

Around 7.00 AM, February 28, I was awakened by some confusion and quick steps resounding in the barracks corridors. It turned out that the march would take place literally within a few minutes, because under the cover of darkness the Russians broke the defensive lines and [entered] Neustettin … *Waffen–Hauptscharführer* Augustin offers me a place in one of the passenger cars. Why not?! Together with two other non-commissioned officers: *Waffen–Scharführer* Marcel and *Waffen–Scharführer* Deligne, we jump inside. The driver moves abruptly, the car with a screech of tyres runs into a street [that has] literally collapsed, with … vehicles, bicycles, soldiers and escaping civilians. Everyone pushes west. We need a slalom to pass the next characters who do not think to give way. Zigzag[ging, we move] forward towards Bärwalde."[47]

---

44 This officer survived the Pomeranian campaign and shortly before the end of the war he found himself with a group of 11 other soldiers of the *33. Waffen-Grenadier-Division der SS* near Bad Reichenhall in Bavaria. They were captured by soldiers of the French 2nd Armoured Division conducting operations alongside the United States Army. After a short interrogation, on 7 May 1945 they eceived a death sentence for treason and were shot on the spot. Among the victims – in addition to *Waffen-Untersturmführer* Daffas – *Waffen-Obersturmführer* Serge Krotoff, who was born in Paris, and *Waffen-Untersturmführer* Paul Briffaut, from Nice, were also identified..

45 R. Forbes, *For Europe…*, pp. 298–300.

46 Por. *Panzerzug, czyli pociąg, który brał udział w walkach o Kołobrzeg*, [w:] 'Głos Kołobrzegu', Friday 12 August 2016 r. (Koszalin: 2016), p. 10.

47 This small group, using only the tourist map of Central Pomerania, managed to reach Barwice (Bärwalde) moving through Trzesiek (Streitzig), Prosinko (Neudorf) and Ostropole (Osterfelde). From there, they continued through Łeknica (Lucknitz), Połczyn Zdrój (Bad Polzin), Buślary (Buslar), Tychówko (Wodlisch Tychow) and Byszyno

At the request of Szczecinek's commanding officer, *Oberst* Arthur Kopp, a rearguard was left in place. This was composed of elements of the 4th Company of the *58. Waffen-Grenadier Regiment der SS* under the command of *Waffen-Obersturmführer* Tardan and the 10th (anti-tank) Company of the same regiment, commanded by *Waffen-Oberscharführer* Girard, as well as an anti-aircraft unit. The first of the above officers, Tardan, was the son of a hatter from Mexico City, and his subordinates used the battle cry: "All Mexicans wear a sombrero from Tardan!" A total of 250 Frenchmen were in the rearguard, which was commanded by a 25-year-old former pilot, *Waffen-Obersturmführer* Michel Auphan, who had previously served as a pilot-instructor with the Polish Air Force in France in 1940. The sector he was assigned to defend was 1.2km long and was located between two battalions of other troops. The northern edge of the post was manned by subordinates of *Waffen-Unstersturmführer* Fayard, and the southern perimeter by Tardan. Meanwhile, an anti-tank group was selected from the 10th Company, armed with *Panzefausts*, to watch for Soviet tanks.

On 28 February, around 1700 hours, the headquarters of the Szczecinek garrison decided to leave the city and establish a new defensive line based on the nearby*Pommernstellung* fortifications. Soviet soldiers eventually took the railway bridge, which was located on today's Pilska Street and National Road 11. When members of the French unit, which had been defending the line for several hours, noticed that the German troops accompanying them began to flee without waiting for the orders of *Oberst* Kopp, they themselves also fell back. Suffering losses, they left in the direction of Połczyn Zdrój, but failed to merge with any other German units. Instead, they found a command post shelled by mortars, probably prepared by the Szczecinek HQ, with scattered maps, documents and even a functional telephone. They decided to head to the nearest place, Trzesieki (Streitzig), located less than 5km to the east. Holding on to the railway line, the division was divided into two columns, commanded by Auphan and Fayard. After suffering several reverses, fighting for almost three days in an area almost entirely controlled by the Russians, they joined other units in Karlino (Körlin). Seven men of this group received battlefield awards of the Iron Cross 2nd Class.[48]

A slightly different version of the events described above was given by *Waffen-Obersturmführer* Tardan in his memoirs, shared with Robert Forbes, author of the book *For Europe: The French Volunteers of the Waffen-SS*. Tardan claimed that when the enemy broke the defences on the road from Szczecinek to Czaplinek (Tempelburg), some of the troops fell into disarray. Consequently, an organized retreat was out of the question, as was any communication with the 10th Company. At around 1800 hours on 28 February, a group of French subordinated to him at the last moment before the victory of the Soviets in this section fled towards Połczyn Zdrój and spent the whole

(Boissin) to Białogard (Belgard an der Persante). *Waffen-Rottenführer* Robert Soulat testimony, p. 12.

48   Among them were *Waffen-Obersturmführer* Tardan and *Waffen-Unstersturmführer* Fayard.

night wandering around. Finally, before noon on 1 March, Tardan joined the rest of *Waffen-Obersturmführer* Auphan's teams. From there, within the next 48 hours or so, chasing after the core of the division, they moved to Białogard and Karlino.

Sczecinek (Neustettin) railway station in March 2017, from where, on 27 February 1945, the *33. Waffen-Grenadier Division der SS Charlemagne* started its retreat from the city. (Photo Łukasz Gładysiak)

Jean Mabire, author of the 2005 book *La Division Charlemagne*, sheds further light on events involving the anti-aircraft company of *Waffen-Unstersturmführer* Fayard, which in the defence of Szczecinek lost almost half of its number over several hours of hard fighting. The unit was to leave the city overnight from 28 February to 1 March, using railroad transport. Earlier, under cover of darkness, Mabire wrote that they found a locomotive ready for departure, which they armed with their own firearms. Thus, they shot their way out of the city.[49]

The marching out of the infantry column of the division began at 0700 hours on 28 February, with the 2nd Battalion *58. Waffen-Grenadier Regiment der SS* bringing

---

49   J. Mabire, *La Division Charlemagne sur le front de l'est* (Paris: 2005), pp. 395–96. In the author's opinion, this thesis looks too fantastic to be true.

up the rear. A group of French prisoners of war were captured on the border. They had been taken during the battle for France nearly five years earlier. Ten of them joined the unit. Three-and-a-half hours later, the marching French were hit by the Soviet Air Force, which forced them to return almost to the gates of Szczecinek. Red Army infantry who had pushed deeper into the city became a real danger to them. In addition, after breaking the barricades on the road leading to Czaplinek, being enclosed in the salient became almost certain.[50] Christian La Mazière, who took part in the march to Połczyn Zdrój, described it as follows: "And so we walked madly, freezing, whipped by wind and needles of freezing snow. Breath pressed into the mouth, swelling bubbles twisted the intestines. And around us this relentless silent procession of refugees: insanely silent, ghosts." Near Barwice, the column was attacked once again by Soviet planes.

At this time, the *33. Waffen-Grenadier-Division der SS Charlemagne*, by decision of the authorities in Berlin, was formally subordinated to the staff of the German *3. Panzerarmee*, which was then in Płoty (Plathe), and at lower levels, to the *X SS-Armeekorps* and *Korpsgruppe von Tettau*, commanded by *General der Infanterie* Hans Bernhard von Tettau. The staff of the latter was also heading towards Białogard. Obviously, the French soldiers knew nothing about such events. It was only during the retreat from Szczecinek that many of the division's troops had the chance to replenish their equipment and replace losses incurred in their combat debut. Christian La Mazière has written: "We walked on foot primarily burdened with ammunition. We armed ourselves quickly, grabbing any weapon and ammunition that was around. Thanks to this I had a *Sturmgewehr*. Several ladder carts loaded with weapons followed us."[51]

That well-known health resort of Bad Polzin was just another short-lived stage on the road, which this time headed straight to the north. It seems almost impossible to indicate the exact route taken to Białogard through Parsęta and Liśnica today. The most likely seems to be along forest paths running along the current Voivodship Road 163. This is confirmed by the account of one of the witnesses of the final march, in which it is said that a few kilometres from Białogard, the French column was seen by *Wehrmacht* forces riding in the same direction.[52]

If the above statement is true, the next points on the route would be the villages of: Ostre Bardo (Wusterbarth), Osówko (Wutzow) and Byszyno (Boissin). At this stage, the partial dispersion of the group and radio communication problems became evident.[53] A snow storm, which lasted for most of the journey, did not make things easier. The march, which was led by the 7th Company of the *58. Regiment* under the command of *Waffen-Haupsturmführer* Eric Walter, had as its rearguard the regiment's

50   Ibid., pp. 292–95.
51   Ch. de La Mazière, *Marzyciel w...*, p. 75.
52   R. Forbes, *For Europe...*, p. 297.
53   J. Mabire, *La Division...*, p. 393.

10th Company, led by *Waffen-Oberscharführer* Girard, and took place under the cover of night to minimize the risk of detection and attacks by Soviet aviation operating freely over the central part of Pomerania. The Great War veteran, *Waffen-Hauptsturmführer* Marc Raoul de Perricot, kept the column in order from horseback.

The soldiers became more and more tired as extreme fatigue set in. Morale weakened by the hour. The situation was not improved by the news of the death of the French fascist sympathizer Jacques Doriot, who fell on 22 February during German artillery shelling in the vicinity of the city of Mengen in Germany. There were also cases of dysentery. Brothers-in-arms sought to raise the spirits of *Waffen-Oberführer* Puaud, who gave up travelling by car and marched with his men, sometimes carrying a 7.92mm *Maschinengewehr 42* machine gun over his shoulder. As Christian La Mazière remembered, the general used to say: "I pulled you into all this, but I will get you out of here, I promise."

The 'long march' of more than 30km by the veterans came to an end on 1 March at about 0600 hours on the southeastern edge of Białogard. La Mazière noted: "Finally, a stop order. We fell on the snow in the glaciated forest. Those who still had tent sheets began to clip them into pyramids. We enjoyed total inertia for several minutes. Hunger pulled us out of it."[54]

Gruß aus Belgard an der Persante

Białogard (Belgard an der Persante) – another point on the *Charlemagne* Division's route – as seen on a postcard from the mid-war era. (Studio Historyczne Huzar Archive)

54   Ch. de La Mazière, *Marzyciel w...*, pp. 77–78.

It is hard to say where exactly the *Charlemagne* Division stopped. Based on the memories of veterans quoted by Robert Forbes in his book, two locations are seriously considered. The first of them could be somewhere near the village of Rzyszczewo (Ristow), the other the crossroads of today's provincial roads 163 and 169 in Przegonia (Heidekrug). Another hypothesis points to a small settlement called Sternkrug, located next to Rogowo (Roggow), whose existence is confirmed by German district censuses. It cannot be ruled out that veterans may have misread the name of the village, so Moczyłki (Springkrug) could also be the site. Whatever the case, *SS-Brigadeführer* Krukenberg and the divisional HQ officers moved by cars from Koczała (Flötenstein) via Bobolice and Koszalin,[55] and finally reached Byszyno, where they were temporarily settled in one of the manors.[56] There was finally time for some control and reorganization of the survivors.

It is worth noting that the march north from Połczyn Zdój did not go without losses. In a shop located in Rąbino (Gross Rambin), it seems a military first aid point for soldiers of other German units was installed. Two seriously wounded members of the *58. Waffen-Grenadier Regiment der SS* and four of their comrades from *57. Regiment* were sent there. All of them died. Their corpses were left behind by the retreating Germans. Another version says that they were shot on the spot by the Soviets after the village was taken. It is possible that these French soldiers lost their lives a little later, after the final retreat of the *Charlemagne* Division from Białogard. They may have belonged to one of the small detachments captured by Soviet or Polish forces (the 1st Polish Army was also operating in the area, heading towards Kołobrzeg) while trying to break through enemy lines.

55   The route was confirmed by *Waffen-Rottenführer* Robert Soulat in a letter sent to author in September 2011.
56   R. Forbes, *For Europe...*, p. 297.

4

Death of the Division

Founded in the 13th century, the fortified city of Białogard[1] did not have much strategic significance for the German Army. In addition to the Germania parquet factory, three breweries, a dairy and a factory, which were otherwise valued throughout Germany and much of Europe, the city was devoid of industry. Its obvious advantage was the large railway junction, with facilities for wagons and locomotives. The military infrastructure, however, developed in the second half of the 1930s, was significant. With the establishment of the staff of the German *32. Infantrie-Division* in Koszalin in October 1936, as well as the dynamic development of this formation's sub-units in all major cities of central Pomerania on the Parsęta and Liśnica rivers, two barracks complexes were built: at today's Zwycięstwa Street (*Von Scholz Kaserne*) and Połczyńska Chausse (*Von Hindersin Kaserne*). Originally, these were intended for the division's 32nd measurement squadron and elements of the 68th heavy artillery regiment, respectively. The *Wehrmacht* also had barracks put into use at the beginning of the 20th century in Kołobrzeska Street (*Husaren Kaserne*, also called *Artillerie Kaserne*). In addition, there was a large hospital and warehouse facilities in the city,[2] so in all there was much military activity in and around the city.

From 20 January 1945, when the Gneisenau Alarm had been announced for the entire 2nd Military District, residents of Białogard, like the German population in other Pomeranian towns, were awaiting an evacuation signal. It is estimated that their number, taking into account refugees arriving almost every day from other parts of the region, could have reached over 20,000.[3] Defensive preparations were started. According to the latest military orders, there were more and more *Volkssturm* members

---

1   The fortified villa Alba (the very first name of Białogard) existed long before that date. It is mentioned in early medieval sources, having the status of one of the major political and military centres of the mid-Pomeranian region.

2   'Lwia głowa' w Białogardzie, [w:] 'Głos Koszaliński/Głos Koszalina', Friday 9 January 2015 r. (Koszalin: 2015), p. 11.

3   Cz. Partacz, Wyzwolenie Białogardu, [w:] Białogard 1299–1999. Studia z dziejów miasta (Białogard: 1999), p. 141.

visible around the city. They were acompanied by a group of Russian Liberation Army (ROA), whose presence in the city still needs confirmation. With Soviet manoeuvres suggesting that the attack would probably be launched from the east and south – from Pomianowo (Pumlow), Żytelkowo (Siedkow) and Dębczyno (Denzin) – field fortifications and wooden anti-tank obstacles were installed on the main roads in those sectors.[4]

Though disturbing reports were received, mostly about the Red Army's bloody retaliation against the German civilian population, the danger of the approaching front was generally not felt. Otto Holznagel, a shopkeeper called up to serve in Białogard with the *374. Grenadier-Bataillon-Ersatz* (374th Replacement Grenadier Battalion), noted in his diary: "The impending danger officially did not seem to be noticed by representatives of the high-ranking members of the of the National Socialist German Workers' Party – NSDAP. In the first days of March 1945, posters were hung on advertising poles that there was no threat from the Red Army, and all residents should, as before, fulfill their duties."[5]

The entry of the *33. Waffen-Grenadier Division der SS Charlemagne* into the city on the Parsęta and Liśnica rivers on 1 March 1945 could have take place along two routes. The first, entirely coinciding with the course of today's Voivodship Road 163, ran through Przegonia and Moczyłki, passing the massive buildings of *Von Hindersin Kaserne*. At the base of the second possible route was the assumption that the starting point was around Rogowo. After crossing the bridge over the Parsęta and passing on the left side of the Białogard dairy, they would entered Kisielice Duże Street straight into the city centre.

Other than the main group, in late February and early March 1945, single soldiers or smaller units of the *Charlemagne* Division also appeared in the city. In the ranks of one of these groups was *Waffen-Rottenführer* Soulat, who remembered the first, and only as it turned out, moments of his stay as follows:

> Finally Belgard – a nice, quiet-looking town with about fifteen thousand inhabitants. In the centre of the road our car [travelled on], a gendarme with a characteristic gorge on a chain hung on the chest [rose up in front of us]. Waving a red lollipop, he ordered [us] to pull over. Our driver, initially reducing speed, suddenly [stepped on the] gas. The surprised gendarme opens his mouth wide when we [look at him], rushing towards Köslin.[6]

The first hours of the groups' stay in the city were spent mainly in searching for food. Some, if you believe the memories of veterans, took advantage of the opportunity to

---

4   Ł. Gładysiak, *Belgard w rękach Sowietów*, 'Głos Koszalina', Friday 6 March 2015 (Koszalin: 2015), p. 11.
5   *Otto Holznagel from Belgard memoires*, published on *Altes Land Belgard* website.
6   *Waffen-Rottenführer* Roberta Soulat testimony..., p. 13.

Aerial photo of Białogard (Belgard an der Persante) taken in the 1930s. This was the location of the *Charlemagne* Division's reorganization. (Studio Historyczne Archive)

bathe in barracks, most likely in *Von Hindersin Kaserne*. Christian La Mazière recalled how one of his companions organized a hunt, shooting several animals and taking them to a collection point. The staff were furious at his actions, and the guilty fellow was called to be immediately judged and sentenced to death for insubordination. Instead of the soldier, however, it is said that a puppet stood before the firing squad!

La Mazière also observed the first meeting with the locals: "I took a few soldiers and went to Belgard. The few civilians who remained here welcomed us [in a] friendly [manner], but the city was almost completely [empty]."[7] This comment, however, seems to be inconsistent with the reality of the situation. By 1 March, life in Białogard was obviously affected by the proximity of the Soviet spearheads. Otto Holznagel, a soldier of the city's garrison, recalled: "On March 3, around 1:00 PM I left the artillery barracks [at today"s Kołobrzeska Street, but then *Koerliner Strasse*] and guided by *Friedrichstrasse* [now Wojska Polskiego Street] I got to my apartment at *Hindenbrugstrasse* [1 Maja Street]. Traffic on the streets was normal. We waited in suspense for what the next days or even hours would bring."[8] Although Holznagel refers to a time when the *33. Waffen-Grenadier Division der SS* was no longer in Białogard, it can be presumed that in previous days the situation must have been

7   Ch. de La Mazière, *Marzyciel w...*, p. 78.
8   *Otto Holznagel from Belgard memoires...*

similar. The alarm for civilians to leave the city immediately was not announced until 3 March at 1800 hours.

The first day of the new month was one of the most important in the French unit's short history. Due to the losses incurred by the end of February, orders were issued for its reorganization. Although, according to *Wehrmacht* regulations, such activities should take about 48 hours, the risk of a renewed confrontation with the Red Army forced them to be carried out in just 10 hours. Following the French military tradition, the soldiers were divided into two newly created regiments. The first – the Marching Regiment, or *SS-Marsch Regiment 33* (in the native language of the soldiers simply the *Régiment de Marche*), whose command was given to *Waffen-Sturmbannführer* Emile Raybaud – received the most valuable armament: machine guns, *Panzerfausts* and *RpZB 43* or *RBzP 54* missile launchers (so-called *Panzerschrecks*)[9], a few mortars, as well as two 75mm anti-tank guns formerly belonging to the 9th Company of the *57. Waffen-Grenadier Regiment der SS*. There were also 600 soldiers gathered in two battalions, the first led by *Waffen-Obersturmführer* Henri Fenet and the second by *Waffen-Hauptsturmführer* Jean Basompierre. The second 'new' regiment, the *SS-Reserve Regiment 33* (or *Régiment de Reserve*), was commanded by *Waffen-Sturmbannführer* Victor de Bourmont. This also had two battalions, commanded by *Waffen-Hauptsturmführer* Emile Monneuse and *Waffen-Hautpsturmführer* Maurice Berrett. There were also unarmed or only partly armed soldiers, the wounded and those who had declared no motivation to fight. The new organization of the division, along with the identifiable commanders of individual sub-units, is included in one of the tables in Appendix I.

The assignment to a particular regiment, battalion or company was often decided by the individual case or the wishes of the soldier. Many of the Frenchmen, binding their hopes for the future with a kind of heroic divisional cult, reported to their old command, disregarding their new official assignments. Christian La Mazière, from 1 March 1 an officer in the 2nd Battalion of the *Régiment de Marche*, commented on the reorganization in Białogard: "I felt like [I was] on the school pitch during a break when collecting volunteers to kick the ball."[10] It was probably at this time that *Waffen-Oberführer* Puaud officially announced for the first time the possibility of an arbitrary evacuation of elements to Kołobrzeg. A group of 300 Frenchmen opted to go there as soon as possible.[11] Finally, some 2,700 French *Waffen-SS* troops composed the division, or rather the core of it. About 1,200 of them were assigned to *SS-Marsch Regiment 33*,[12] which seemed to be the only unit prepared to fight the Soviets.

9   Występowanie tej broni w Pułku Marszowym potwierdził *Waffen-Rottenführer* Robert Soulat. List Roberta Soulata do autora z dnia 3 sierpnia 2011 roku. Rękopis w zbiorach autora

10   Ch. de La Mazière, *Marzyciel w hełmie...*, p. 78.

11   L. Saint-Loup, *Les hérétiques* (Paris: 1965), p. 266.

12   R. Forbes, *For Europe...*, p. 300.

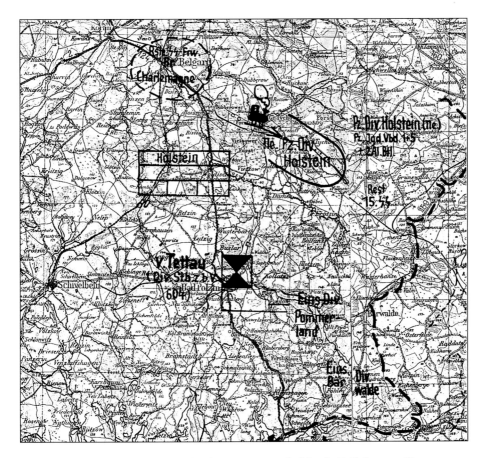

Part of a *Heeresgruppe Weichsel* headquarters map of 1 March 1945 showing German positions. The *Charlemagne* Division's positions are in the upper sector. (United States National Archives)

On the same day, around 1800 hours, *SS-Brigadeführer* Krukenberg was instructed to go to Karlino, 8km north of Białogard.[13] Karlino, located on one of the main Pomeranian crossroads connecting the route from Szczecin to Gdańsk and Kołobrzeg to Piła, was ordered to be prepared for long-term defence. The Soviet advance guard reached Świdwin (Schivbelbein) and prepared to launch an attack northwards to the sea.

The departure for new positions had to start immediately. Troops were ordered to take only basic equipment – armament with the maximum amount of ammunition

<hr/>

13   J. Mabire, *La Division…*, p. 411. According to Robert Forbes, the event took place 24 hours later.

and basic food rations. Some also managed to get warm clothes from local civilians.[14] Assigned to *Waffen-Hauptsturmfürer* Basompierre's group, Christian La Mazière recalled: "We had taken as many infantry weapons as was possible. *Mauser* rifles and *StG 44* assault rifles hit our backs sideways, weighing us down mercilessly. The heaviest was the *MG42* machine gun, which, together with the ammunition belts, weighed 20kg. We supported each other. There were no more military ranks, no hierarchy.".

They marched by way of Kołobrzeska Street, passing the bridge over the railroad, *Husaren Kaserne*, the cemetery and then the villages of Trzebiele (Komet) and Redlino (Redlin) on the course of the modern Provincial Road 163. The column was led by the best-armed members of the *Marsch Regiment*. Its tail included horse-drawn carts of the *Régiment de Reserve*. Helmut Lindenblatt, the author of a 2008 book describing the Pomeranian campaign of 1945, claimed that a small group of French SS-men took a short break in Lulewice (Alt Lülfitz).[15] This sounds doubtful, because the village is about 4km east of the main route taken by the troops. However, the group could have been soldiers trying to reach the Baltic coast on their own.

The exodus of the *33. Waffen-Grenadier der SS Charlemagne* from Białogard took place at a time appropriate for each individual. On 2 March, in the so-called 'Schivelbein Pocket' – where units including the *X SS-Armeekorps* led by *Generalleutnant* Günther Krappe were surrounded – the Red Army began another offensive. During the day, Soviet tanks bypassed the city, and the vanguard of the 1st Guards Tank Army, under the command of General Mikhail Katukov, reached the Baltic near Łazy (Laase). The attack on the area where the French were reorganizing, supported by artillery fire near Kamosowo (Kamissow) and Nasutowo (Natztow), began on the afternoon of 4 March. On the same day, Koszalin fell into the hands of the Soviets. Red Army tanks and armoured cars approached from the villages of Buczek (Butzke) and Pomianowo (Pumlow), entering the city for the first time around 2100 hours. Apart from sporadic resistance around the Zwycięstwa Street barracks and Schleeberg heights,[16] as well as the railroad station and *Parkettenfabrik* factory, there was no significant fighting in Białogard. The Soviets' advantage was so overwhelming that by 5 March, the city had been taken with minimal losses.[17]

In describing the exit of the *Charlemagne* Division from the city on the Liśnica and Parsęta rivers, it is worth recalling that at least a dozen of its soldiers reached Koszalin at this time. This group included *Waffen-Rottenführer* Soulat, who, together

---

14   H. Lindenblatt, *Pommern 1945. Eines der letzten Kapitel in der Geschichte vom Untergant des Dritten Reiches* (Würzburg: 2008), p. 217.

15   Ibid., p. 255.

16   The Schleeberg heights is an area of Zwycięstwa Street and the exit to Pomianowo and Buczek villages.

17   Ł. Gładysiak, *Belgard w rękach...*, p. 11. Soviet commanders reported that there had been a fierce struggle for Białogard. They also said that there were 1,300 German soldiers defending the city, suported by 14 tanks, neither of which was true.

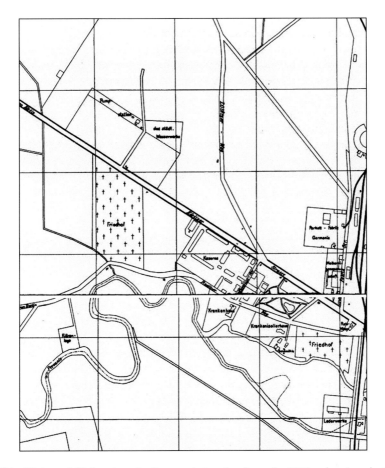

Part of the Białogard (Belgard an der Persante) city plan from the 1930s, showing the former *Körlinerstrasse* (today's Kołobrzeska Street). In March 1945, it was the route taken by the *Charlemagne* Division, as well as one of the reatreating points of Henri Fenet's unit a few days later. (Studio Historyczne Huzar Archive)

with *Waffen-Hauptscharführer* Augustin and three other Frenchmen, arrived in the city by car on the afternoon of 28 February. Soulat recalled:

> We drive slowly down the street, along the column of marching Hungarian soldiers in rotten green uniforms. In the courtyard of the barracks [most likely the barracks at today's 4 Marca Street] *Wehrmacht* soldiers hurriedly release weapons and gas masks. We look at this human anthill leaning on the hood of the car. Suddenly: anti-aircraft alarm! We run to the shelter. After about half an hour, going outside, I meet my close friend from the time of service in

the *Kriegsmarine* – Gegenea Vaulot,[18] actually *Waffen-Unterscharführer* of the Replacement Company in our division. He is accompanied by over a dozen other Frenchmen. They say that they arrived here after losing contact with their parent unit whose transport was bombed by Soviet aircraft near Altdamm. Shortly afterwards, several *Charlemagne* cars enter the barracks main square.

A few divisional military police appeared in the column of troops. They said the troops were needed at Białogard to strengthen the French unit there, which caused the chaotic dislocation to begin. Today we can be sure that one of the locations passed through during the French route was Nosowo, where the soldiers took a break during the night of 28 February/1 March. Waffen-Rottenführer Soulat recalled meeting with villagers there:

> It is around 3.00 in the morning. We enter the yard of a nice-looking farm with a barn, which looms before us like a lost paradise. In the corner, the local farmer probably argues loudly with one of our NCOs. 'I don't want to hear about any uniformed accommodation. When it is my turn to ask for accommodation?' He looks at me like a stray dog. He would probably kick me away. In the face of categorical refusal, we move to another farm. The old, moustached owner stands with his back against the frontage of the house and, as we have got used to, looks at us crookedly. I take an unopened packet of cigarettes from my pocket; it convinces him. We roll into the yard. A large barn is literally bursting at the seams with civilian refugees crammed everywhere. There seems to be no place for us, but the moustache man throws two bundles of hay onto the floor. We jumped into it willingly.

The group continued its march at 0600 hours. About three hours later, it reached the centre of Białogard, probably what is nowadays Wolności Square. From there, the troops started looking for their comrades, with whom they finally moved northwards.[19]

Author Richard Landwehr has stated that the commander of *Heeresgruppe Weichsel*, *Reichsführer-SS* Heinrich Himmler himself, ordered that Karlino be defended to the last bullet.[20] Located on the Radew and Parsęta river crossing, Karlino was one of the most important defensive position on the route to Kołobrzeg. The struggle for Karlino, despite making no sense strategically, could surely slow down enemy units then gathered near Świdwin (Schivelbein) – the Red Army – and Sławoborze (Stolzenberg) – 1st Polish Army.

---

18   Osobą, o której wspomina autor relacji był *Waffen-Unterscharführer* Eugène Vaulot, jeden z bohaterów 33. Dywizji Grenadierów SS *Charlemagne*, zwłaszcza w kontekście późniejszych walk o Berlin, i kawaler Krzyża Rycerskiego Żelaznego Krzyża – patrz: Aneks I.

19   *Waffen-Rottenführer* Robert Soulat testimony..., pp. 15–16.

20   R. Landwehr, *French Volunteers...*, p. 46.

The former German barracks at 4 Marca Street in Koszalin (Köslin) in March 2017. Accordung to *Waffen-Rottenführer* Robert Soulat's testiomony, a group of French *Waffen-SS* soldiers were gathered there for a short time on 28 February 1945. (Photo Łukasz Gładysiak)

It was originally intended that the March Regiment of the *Charlemagne* Division be established in the centre of Karlino, with the Reserve Regiment watching the situation around the bridges over the Parsęta and Radew. Under the command of *Waffen-Obersturmführer* Henri Fenet, the 1st Battalion of the *Régiment de Marche* set off southwards, eventually manning outposts in Redlino. Meanwhile, the 2nd Battalion blocked the exit from the city towards Krzywopłoty (Stadtholzkathen) and Koszalin. On a wide section of the front, running along the eastern bank of the Parsęta, there were disarmed platoons of the Reserve Regiment. The northernmost point which the soldiers had to guard was near Miechęcino (Mechentin), more than 16km from the centre of the coming battle. The 2nd Company of the 1st Battalion crossed the river and entered Piotrowice (Peterfitz).[21] The 2nd Battalion of the *Régiment de Reserve*, whose exhausted commander *Waffen-Hauptsturmführer* Maurice Berret was replaced by *Waffen-Untersturmführer* Michel de Genouillac,[22] was installed in positions in what is now Nadbrzeżna Street, protecting the railway bridge over the Radew River. The

---

21   R. Forbes, *For Europe…*, p. 303.
22   Ibid., p. 307.

upper floor of the lineman house and the Hotel Zur Eisenbahn on Koszalińska Street were chosen for observation points.

The Lineman house and Hotel Zur Eisenbahn in Karlino (Körlin) in March 2017 which in the first days of March 1945 were chosen for observation points by the 2nd Battalion of the Reserve Regiment. This was also the place of the last meeting of *Waffen-Oberführer* Edgar Puaud before his withdrawal from the city. (Photo Łukasz Gładysiak).

The staff of *SS-Brigadeführer* Krukenberg was located in the classical palace of the von Gaudecker family in Karścino (Kerstin), about 7.5km northwest of Karlino. Initially, the anti-tank company of the former *57. Waffen-Grenadier Regiment der SS* was positioned there, but it was sent to strengthen the positions in the city. On 2 March, *Waffen-Hauptsturmführer* Marc Raoul de Perricot was appointed as adjutant to the division commander, with the forces in Karlino commanded by *Waffen-Sturmbanführer* Emile Raybaud, which, considering his nationality, was an unprecedented situation in the armed forces of the Third Reich. Their headquarters became the city hall, where some of the rooms were taken by officers of the 2nd Marching Battalion under *Waffen-Hauptsturmführer* Jean Basompierre.

Other outposts were established in Kowańcz (Kowanz). As the local HQ and first aid point, a huge manor house that belonged to an NSDAP member was chosen. There was also a supply column park there, with carts to be used to tow the division's last operational guns. *Waffen Hauptsturmführer* Bisiau and his forces from Gryfice were ordered to defend the village. It was one of three groups numbering more than

Von Gaudecker's palace in Karścino (Kerstin) in an early 20th-century postcard. It was the headquarters of the *Charlemagne* Division from 1–3 March 1945. (Studio Historyczne Huzar Archive)

100 French soldiers which had not participated in the fighting so far. All support forces were led by *Waffen-Haupsturmführer* Remy and, under orders from the German portion of the divisional staff, the Swiss-born *SS-Obersturmführer* Ludwig. Before the soldiers reached the Parsęta and Radew river crossing, they moved through Trzebiatów (Treptow an der Rega) and Kołobrzeg (Kolbrzeg),[23] from where they were sent 17km south to Gościno (Gross Jestin) before marching to Karlino and being divided into three independent, company-strength combat groups. In addition to the unit which was sent to Kowańcz, the formation commanded by *Waffen-Untersturmführer* Pignard-Berthet most likely went to Karścino as *SS-Brigadeführer* Krukenberg's bodyguard. Two more units, commanded by *Waffen-Obersturmführer* de Bregeot and *Waffen-Hauptsturmführer* Flemish, joined the 1st and 2nd Battalion of *SS-March Regiment 33* respectively.[24]

One of the key tasks of the group's staffs and sub-units accompanying them was to ensure communication between the French units scattered over a relatively large space. This task was hampered by poor weather conditions and the activities of Soviet

23   L. Saint-Loup, *Les hérétiques...*, p. 273.
24   R. Forbes, *For Europe...*, p. 305.

scouts and local saboteurs, including French and Polish forced laborers who regularly damaged German telephone lines.[25] At the same time, attempts were made to gather under uniform command the remaining soldiers in Karlino. To this end, armed patrols prevented *Wehrmacht* survivors from escaping from the city. Unexpectedly, however, the problem arose that not all Germans recognized their subordination to French commanders, often ignoring their orders. Christian La Mazière recalled that one of them, commanding a platoon-strength unit, refused to join the rest of the hastily created garrison, instead fleeing the city and heading for Kołobrzeg. In the following weeks, the news of this insubordination reached the staff of *Heeresgruppe Weichsel*. At the request of *Reichsführer-SS* Heinrich Himmler himself, the officer was found, degraded, and send to the ranks of the *33. Waffen-Grenadier Division der SS Charlemagne* in April 1945.

Some of the division's soldiers started to erect improvised, mostly wooden obstacles. Robert Forbes has suggested that there was a small amphibious military vehicle at the disposal of the *Charlemagne* Division, driven by *Waffen-Rottenführer* Gonzales from the 2nd Battalion of the Régiment de Marche to patrol the Parsęta and Radew rivers. If true, it was probably a *Volkswagen Typ 166*, the so-called *Schwimmwagen*.[26] Others tried to refill supplies, especially food. *Waffen-Rottenführer* Sepchant visited a grocery, but the shopkeeper refused to give him anything because the French did not have ration cards issued by the local civil authorities.[27]

A pause in the fighting of almost three days was not enough to significantly increase the morale of the survivors of the *Charlemagne* Division. Often extremely tired, they presented a spectacle far from the ideal defender of European civilization promoted by National Socialist propaganda at the beginning of 1945. *Waffen-Rottenführer* Soulat noted in his memoirs:

> My colleagues dressed [in an] extremely 'motley' [fashion]. Some wrapped themselves in camouflage tent curtains thrown on their coats, others, as if they did not feel cold, paraded in only sweatshirts and with rolled-up sleeves. You can probably find all the headgear encountered at that time in the German army: from steel helmets used by the minority through civilian fur hats and field hats with visors. One of our comrades, with machine gun straps slung obliquely across his chest, even tied an ordinary scarf in a truly pirate style. Anyway, this pretty posture grenadier does not seem to feel cold at all, he unzipped his sweatshirt halfway. People in the city turn away at our sight; the dogs howl.[28]

---

25   R. Landwehr, *French Volunteers...*, p. 62.
26   According to Waffen-Rottenführer Robert Soulat memories, small, German amphibious vehicle had been taken by French in Szczecinek [Neustettin]. See also: R. Forbes, *For Europe...*, p. 308.
27   Ibidem, s. 303.
28   Waffen-Rottenführer testimony..., p. 17.

Analyzing the state of preparation of the French division to defend Karlino, there is one unsolved mystery. Christian La Mazière mentioned that a tank was used by those defending the city,[29] and Robert Forbes agreed with him.[30] It is hard to say whether or not during the short battle for the city any German tracked vehicle was used. It could have been that a single *Panzerkampfwagen IV Ausf. H* medium tank appeared in Karlino. One such vehicle was assigned at the beginning of March 1945 to *Panzergruppe Beyer* – an improvised German armoured unit formed as an element of the *Festung Kolberg* garrison.[31] Its crew could have driven the tank from the south through the French defensive positions, but this is only the author's suggestion and requires verification. The truth is that the *Charlemagne* Division at this time had in its arsenal two 75mm towed guns, probably for anti-tank purposes. One of these was deployed on the Białogardzka Street bridge at the Radew strongpoint facing the Redlino road.

The bridge over the Radew in Karlino (Körlin), in Białogardzka Street, in March 2017. A 75mm anti-tank gun was used there by the French *Waffen-SS* soldiers during the struggle for city. Before leaving their position, *Charlemagne* engineers installed explosives under the bridge, which were only found and disarmed in 2001. (Photo Łukasz Gładysiak)

29 Ch. de La Mazière, *Marzyciel w…*, p. 80.
30 R. Forbes, *For Europe…*, p. 310.
31 The tank was abandoned on Ludwik Waryński Street and Św. Jan Paweł II Alee in Kołobrzeg [Kolberg] in last days of siege. Gładysiak Łukasz, „*Czwórka" z Twierdzy Kołobrzeg*, [w:] „Głos Kołobrzegu", friday 11 September 2015 r., Koszalin 2015, p. 8.

The defence of Karlino against the advancing from Sławoborze of the spearhead of the Soviet 1st Guards Tank Army, commanded by General Mikhail Katukov, began on 3 March at about 1300 hours. Five hours later, *SS-Brigadeführer* Krukenberg's staff received information about the concentration of large enemy forces in the area. It was estimated that as many as 90 tanks and two full regiments of well-armed infantry could fall on the French positions. On the night of 3/4 March, the Soviets approached Gościno and Kołobrzeg. The spectre of encirclement hung over the Karlino garrison. Consequently, a shortening of the defensive lines began on the section occupied by the 1st Battalion of the *Régiment de Marche* around Miechęcino and Piotrowice. The second of these villages, garrisoned by the men of *Waffen-Obersturmführer* Ivan Bartolomei, was abandoned for fear of being completely cut off from other elements of the division. The experienced commander of the 2nd Company decided to dissolve his unit, ordering them to break through in small groups towards the Baltic.[32] Some of the French *SS*-men, including *Waffen-Obersturmführer* Bartolomei himself, decided to move in the opposite direction, heading for Karlino. The next day, they linked up with comrades from *SS-Reserve Regiment 33*.

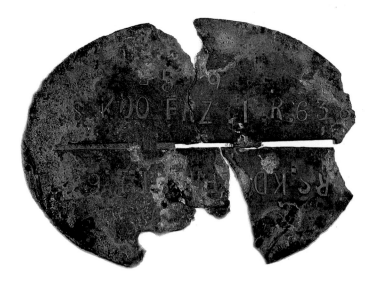

The *Erkennungsmarke* (dog tag) of a *33. Waffen-Grenadier Division der SS Charlemagne* soldier found on the bridge across the Radew in Karlino (Körlin). Note that the date of issue is 1941, so the owner had been an LVF veteran. (Maciej Cichecki Collection)

32   R. Forbes, *For Europe...*, p. 308.

Simultaneously, the sub-unit deployed to Kowańcz attempted to contact the divisional headquarters. A reconnaissance group was sent to the palace in Karścino. The search for the HQ was described by a member of the recon team, *Waffen-Rottenführer* Soulat:

> I volunteer to perform this task. I put the collar [up], unbutton the hat to the covered position to protect the face as much as possible. I take the haversack, rifle, gloves and I'm ready to leave. The road we are taking is completely [covered] in snow. Visibility is limited to only ten metres, a strong wind blows, whose strength, I thought, is constantly increasing. I kept my gloved hands in my coat pockets, but they were still cold. After two hours of Dante's struggle with the elements we arrived at the palace in Karścino. It's half a palace, half a farm. In the room on the ground floor, where the pool table is set, I meet about ten French people. Mostly they are messengers-liaison officers. They lie in the corners on the straw or sit, leaning against the walls. They consider the situation under the strict eye of some Prussian officer from the time of Frederick II, in a monocle and a powdered wig, who, peeking from the picture, is probably very surprised by the whole performance.[33]

As it turned out, the reconnaissance team arrived several dozen minutes late. Due to the threat of being cut off from the remaining elements of the division, *SS-Brigadeführer* Krukenberg and his officers moved the command post 12km north to the now defunct palace in Wrzosowo (Fritzow). At the same time, *Waffen-Untersturmführer* Pignard-Berthet's combat group was divided into smaller units, some of which were sent to Płoty, Kołobrzeg and Świdwin in order to establish contact with the German *III Panzerkorps*. One of the patrols that set off on the night of 3 March encountered, in the vicinity of Świdwin, the *24. Waffen-Grenadier Regiment der SS*, consisting mainly of Danes.[34]

On the morning of 4 March, the Soviet advance guard appeared at the intersection of today's National Road 6 and Provincial Road 163, bypassing the positions of the 1st Battalion of the March Regiment in Redlino. If you believe the words of Christian de la Mazière, the crews of Soviet tanks used a group of refugees as human shields:

> Two tanks push through the fleeing and shoot over their heads. To open the way, soldiers shoot people ... with machine guns. [There is] indescribable panic. Civilians, terrified, are distracted, jump into the river. A moment later, as a result of the explosion of an explosives supply ..., the barricade that blocked the entrance to the city along Białogardzka Street was destroyed. Shrapnel also

33   Ł. Gładysiak, *Francuscy SS-mani w Karścinie*, [w:] 'Głos ma Historia', 25 November 2013 r. (Koszalin: 2013), pp. 8–9. The article had been prepared referring to *Waffen-Rottenführer* Robert Soulat's testimony.
34   R. Forbes, *For Europe...*, p. 312.

The ruins of Von Gaudecker's palace in Karścino (Kerstin) in 2016 – the location of the *Charlemagne* Division's headquarters between 2 and 4 March 1945. (Photo Łukasz Gładysiak)

struck another group of residents of Karlin and refugees. The soldier quoted above noted later: 'Just before me – a gutted Mercedes wreck. Beside some half-naked body, something vibrates in an outstretched hand. We jumped. It was a young woman with a three-year-old child. She protected her from any wounds. Blood seeped from everywhere. I grabbed the baby, two boys took care of the woman. We moved her to my quarters, [and] undressed [her]. [She was] punched like a [sieve], everywhere full of blood ... She was still talking, she wanted to see her daughter. We did that shortly before she died.

In the western part of the city, an attempt to break through to the centre was made by a Soviet patrol, which reach what is now the church of Saint Michael the Archangel. Christian la Mazière also described how the French dealt with this group of Soviet troops:

> I take a few people, we approach the church. The door is closed, [so] I blow it with a grenade. There are shadows behind the columns. They run into the choir and shoot. One Panzerfaust [is] shot at the altar, [there is an] explosion, everything goes up in flames. [There is] some [movement] in the belfry. [After] several [bursts] from automatic weapons and Panzerfausts into the organs they fall apart with a metallic whack. Bodies fall underfoot. A good ten armed troops.[35]

However, this tale seems strongly colourized. Analysis of the destruction of the original church conducted by the author, based on information collected by the priest of the Karlino parish, Ludwik Musiał, indicates that inside there were no signs of damage that a grenade launcher missile would have caused. The organs were also almost completely preserved.[36]

To strenghten his men's morale, Krukenberg himself arrived in Karlino. The city commander, *Waffen-Sturmbanführer* Raybaud, also appeared in the front line with a gun in his hands. A few moments later, Raybaud broke a leg during Soviet shelling (it was later amputated). After passing command to *Waffen-Haupsturmführer* Basompierre, assisted by doctors Paul Durandy and Claude Platon, he was evacuated to Kołobrzeg. He managed to take a boat there and escape to the west.[37] In recognition of his duty, he was promoted to *Waffen-Oberstufmbannführer* and given the Iron Cross 1st Class. After the war, he was accused of collaboration by a court in France and sentenced to five years' imprisonment.[38]

35   Ch. de La Mazière, *Marzyciel w...*, pp. 82–84.
36   L. Musiał, *Pod skrzydłami Anioła. Kościół Św. Michała Archanioła w Karlinie ma 500 lat* (Karlino: 2010), p. 59.
37   J. Mabire, *La Division...*, p. 340.
38   R. Landwehr, *French Volunteers...*, p. 63.

St Michael the Archangel church in Karlino (Körlin) in March 2017 – the place of mysterious confrontation between French and Soviet troops described by Christian la Mazière. (Photo Łukasz Gładysiak)

An Iron Cross 2nd Class found in one of the *Charlemagne* Division strongpoints near Karlino (Körlin). (Maciej Cichecki Collection)

At approximately 1230 hours, the Russians renewed their attack, this time striking along what is now Szczecińska Street. Once again, tanks bearing infantry were directed against the French positions. The delay in the attack allowed soldiers commanded at this section by *Waffen-Hauptsturmführer* de Perricot to carry out an evacuation towards the eastern bank of the Parsęta and Episcopal Island. It was also decided to blow up the bridge leading to the riverside granary. Until now, materials regarding Karlin's history attributed the destruction of the crossing to the Russians. However, events in this part of the city were later described by *Waffen-Rottenführer* Sepchant:

> When a German army officer informed our commander that the bridge would be blown immediately, he turned to me and said: 'Tell him I will sooner make his skull explode than let me blow up the crossing while our soldiers are on the other side.' For obvious reasons, I [ignored] the literal translation, telling the officer to wait [setting off] the explosion until everyone returned to our side [of the bridge]. A moment later our comrades joined us. We didn't see any marauders, so [we blew it up].[39]

It was then reported that there were huge enemy forces gathering between Pobłocie Wielkie (Gross Pobloth) and Gościno. Afraid of being cut off, the commander of *SS-Marsch Regiment 33* decided, without informing divisional headquarters, to shorten his defensive line and move to Mierzyn (Alt Martin), less than 5km from Wrzosowo. This manoeuvre opened up the whole left flank to the Soviet and Polish forces.

The Soviets attacked again at 1430 hours, focusing not only on Karlino, but also on Waffen-Hauptsturmführer Fenet's positions in Redlino. However, despite a clear Soviet numerical advantage, the 2nd Company led by *Waffen-Oberscharführer* Lucien Hennecart launched a counterattack. Although the French managed to eject some of the enemy forces, the battalion command decided to retreat north to join their comrades before the ring around the village closed.[40]

At approximately 1800 hours, Krukenberg held a commanders meeting, attended by *Waffen-Oberführer* Puaud, *SS-Standartenführer* Zimmermann, *Waffen-Sturmbannführer* de Vaugelas, *Waffen-Hauptsturmführer* de Perricot, *Waffen-Hauptsturmführer* Schliser, *Waffen-Obersturmführer* Huan and *Waffen-Obersturmführer* Tardan. The commanders were informed about the *Oberkommando des Heeres* (*OKH*) order that the city should be held at all costs and the unrealistic claim that relief would come from the *10. SS-Panzer Division 'Frundsberg'* breaking through to the city from the west. Regardless of this, Krukenberg announced the evacuation of Karlin, which was to be started by the first group of horse-drawn carts heading towards

---

39 R. Forbes, *For Europe...*, p. 310.
40 L. Saint-Loup, *Les hérétiques...*, p. 292.

The village of Redlino (Redlin) on the road between Białogard (Belgard an der Persante) and Karlino (Körlin) in March 2017. On 2 March 1945, the 1st Battalion of *SS-March Regiment 33* took up positions there. (Photo Łukasz Gładysiak).

the Baltic coast. Today, it is claimed that Krukenberg's decision violating the *OKH* directive was connected with the informal consent to retreat expressed by the head of *Heeresgruppe Weichsel, Reichsführer-SS* Heinrich Himmler.[41] Whatever the reason, this only confirms how chaotic was the command structure between units of this army group in February and March 1945.

The evacuation plan divided all forces into three groups. The first group comprised headquarters staff and soldiers of the 1st Battalion of the *Régiment de Marche*, under *Waffen-Obersturmführer* Fenet. The Reserve Regiment was to follow, led by Puaud and de Vaugelas, who had an estimated 3,000 civilian and military personnel. The rearguard was to be the grenadiers of the 2nd Battalion of *SS-March Regiment 33*, commanded by *Waffen-Hauptsturmführer* Basompierre, supported by the last larger-calibre weapons. The latter was to leave no later than one day after the departure of the first group.[42] The French *SS*-men were directed to first head for Białogard, unaware

41   R. Forbes, *For Europe...*, pp. 310–12. Jean Mabire suggests the order to defend Karlino to the last bullet reached *Heeresgruppe Weichsel* simultanaously to the meeting in the city hall. It is possible that there was a problem in passing the order to the *Charlemagne* Division HQ. J. Mabire, *La Division...*, p. 444.
42   R. Landwehr, *French Volunteers...*, p. 67.

that the city had already fallen to the enemy. From there, the groups were to try to reach Rega River, Trzebiatów, Gryfice, Płoty and on to the Oder. Leaders of the sub-units were told to summon scattered patrols as soon as possible and gather the maximum amount of armament and ammunition. What could not be taken should be destroyed. Christian La Mazière recalled that soldiers were prohibited from taking excessive amounts of food. The most seriously injured were also to be left behind. In order to camouflage the evacuation, which was to take place under the cover of night, units were ordered to wrap the hooves of their horses. The original time of departure, which was ultimately missed, was 2300 hours that night.

The divisional staff meeting lasted about an hour. Then, Krukenberg, Zimmermann and *SS-Hauptsturmführer* Jauss of the *Wehrmacht* French Inspectorate went to the positions of the 1st Battalion of *SS-March Regiment 33*, whose officials were absent from the town hall meeting.

Karlino (Körlin) city hall in March 2017, where town commandant *Waffen-Sturmbannführer* Emile Raybaud was based from 2–5 March 1945. Its rooms had been taken over by some officers of *SS-March Regiment 33*, including *Waffen-Haupsturmführer* Jean Basompierre. Early on the morning of 4 March, a senior officers meeting was called there by *SS-Brigadeführer* Gustav Krukenberg. (Photo Łukasz Gładysiak)

Preparations for the retreat could not escape the German residents of Karlino and refugees from other parts of Pomerania. There were dramatic scenes, which were later described by Christian La Mazière:

> Women, especially those whose daughters were eighteen or twenty years old, quickly realized that their last moments had arrived. Hence, a meeting with the French defending their dignity sparked a spontaneous wave of admiration

bordering on worship. And here the unexpected happened: here mothers offered their daughters to us … Women who had no daughters gave up [themselves].[43]

Around 0030 hours, the last train passed through the city, with refugees from Białogard and the surrounding area heading towards the Baltic.[44] During a collection of sub-units organized early in the morning of 5 March, it was found that the number of platoons had decreased by up to half in the previous few hours.[45]

The advance guard of the division set off from Karlino more than a day late. The delay in the evacuation was not only due to the lack of proper organization in the sub-units, but also because of the weather – a cloudless day and clear moonlit night did not favour the French. Eventually, when snow began to fall, Fenet's column and his staff officers, divided into groups of five or six, set off. On 6 March, around 0200, they finally left the city.[46] Passing to the west of the villages of Redlino and Trzebiele, the grouping reached what is today the Olimpijczyków Estate and the S1 Centre shopping complex in Białogard, from where it moved to the edge of the now-non-existent large cemetery at ul. Kołobrzeska. They then moved along Szpitalna Street towards the bend in the Parsęta, which was swum in spite of the cold.[47] Avoiding direct contact with units of the Red Army which were already settled in the city, the French turned southwest and after a 10km march they reached Stanomino (Standemin). The next place on the route of the retreat was more than 25km away, Międzyrzecze (Meseritz). While marching there, the group was forced to move through a concentration of Soviet–Polish forces in Sławoborze. Although they tried to move mainly in the dark, the risk of detection and the possibility of frostbite due to lack of movement meant that the march continued during the daytime, under the cover of forests.

If Robert Forbes, referring to the memories of those who took part, is correct, the column made another turn on 6 March at about 0900 hours, this time to the east. The grenadiers, probably passing the village of Ciechnowo (Technow), crossed the road connecting Rąbino with Białogard, and eventually split into groups of team or platoon strength. The rearguard commanded by Jauss discovered how close the enemy was to them when they ran straight into sleeping Russians while looking for food in one of the abandoned farms. Heading south, the grenadiers went through Jarzębniki (Falkenberg), which had been ravaged by the enemy, and 5km northwest to Słowieńsko Schlenzig), which they reached on 7 March at 0400 hours.

During a three-hour halt, Krukenberg, who was accompanying him, learned from a group of refugees that Gryfice had fallen into the hands of the Red Army. The general

43   Ch. de La Mazière, *Marzyciel w…*, pp. 84–85.
44   The train was stopped by the Soviets on 7 March near Dygowo (Degow). Those who survived the encounter were sent back to Białogard. H. Lindenblatt, *Pommern 1945…*, p. 216.
45   Ch. de La Mazière, *Marzyciel w…*, p. 88.
46   R. Forbes, *For Europe…*, p. 317.
47   Ch. de La Mazière, *Marzyciel w…*, p. 90.

decided not to inform his comrades about this fact, so as not to worsen their already extremely low morale. After covering more than 25km, which separated the resting place from the village of Poradz (Petersfelde) near Łobza (Labes), the group learned about the concentration of larger German forces in the vicinity of Międzyrzecz, from where they set out several hours earlier.[48] Indeed, on 7 March, forces gathered by *Generalmajor* Oskar Munzel were gathered in this part of Pomerania. The core of his improvised battle group was the staff of the 104. Panzer Brigade and elements of the *Führer-Grenadier Division, 163. Infanterie-Division* and *281. Infanterie-Division.*[49]

Extremely exhausted Frenchmen set off back to Międzyrzecze. Wanting to raise the atmosphere in the group, Krukenberg ordered a ceremony during which the *Waffen-Obersturmführer* Fenet was awarded the Iron Cross 1st Class. Because neither the modest resources of the division staff nor the *Korpsgruppe* stores had documents confirming the awarding of the decoration, General Munzel later gave Fenet his own medal.

Shortly afterwards, remnants of the Reserve Regiment reached Międzyrzecze. They managed to escape the massacre near Białogard (see below). This unit of no more than 100 troops was commanded by a former French merchant navy officer, *Waffen-Untersturmführer* Leune. Other officers with him included *Waffen-Obersturmführer* Métais, *Waffen-Obersturmführer* Tardan and *Waffen-Untersturmführer* Herbe. Some of them later recalled that their escape was helped by a Pole encountered along the way, thanks to whom they learned about the location of enemy positions and the occupation of Gryfice, where they were originally heading.

Over the next day, the group was finally disbanded. Some of the soldiers moved arbitrarily westwards. Others, among them *Waffen-Hauptscharführer* Lenoir, *Waffen-Unterscharführer* Deschamps, *Waffen-Unterscharführer* Lhomme, *Waffen-Unterscharführer* Trinqenaux and tailor *Waffen-Oberschüt* Chomy, ditched their uniforms in favour of civilian clothes, and continued their escape.[50] A unified unit led by *Waffen-Untersturmführer* Pignard-Berthet headed for the Oder River, joined by a group of Latvian soldiers from the *15. Waffen-Grenadier Division der SS*. In general, everyone avoided confrontation with the enemy, although according to Robert Forbes, during one skirmish with the Russians, the grenadiers managed to destroy three enemy tanks. On 10 March, the group was finally disarmed and taken to Gryfice as prisoners. The commanding officer himself managed to break free of the column and headed alone towards Płoty. He obtained civilian clothes and introduced himself to Soviet patrols as a chef. It was only when recognized by soldiers of the Polish Army that he was handed it over to the *NKVD* (Soviet secret police).[51]

48   R. Forbes, *For Europe...*, pp. 324–26.
49   W. Tieke, *Tragödie um die Treue. Kampf und Untergang des III (germ.) SS-Panzer-Korps* (Osnabrück: 1978), pp. 168–69.
50   R. Forbes, *For Europe...*, pp. 327–28.
51   Tamże, p. 314.

Two days earlier, hungry and suffering from dysentery, the Frenchmen under the command of Fenet set off towards the Baltic coast. The next day, having established communication with units of *Korps von Tettau*, they reached Rewal (Rewahl).[52]

The largest group, which could have been up to 3,000 strong, was led by Edgar Puaud and began preparations to retreat from Karlino on the evening of 4 March. Using flashlights, in the section occupied by the 2nd Battalion of the Reserve Regiment, efforts were made to collect explosives to blow up a railway viaduct over the Radwia before escaping. What happened then around Dworcowa, Nadbrzeżna and Koszalińska Streets was described by eyewitness *Waffen-Untersturmführer* Michel de Genouillac:

> It was clear to us that if the Russians surprised us during the preparations on the bridge, a catastrophe would occur. The bridge itself was a salvation because it gave a chance to leave the city. The problem was that we should destroy it so that we could cut off the path of a possible pursuit. Theoretically, *Panzerfausts* could be used for this, but we gave them all to comrades from the March Regiment. When General Puaud visited us in the evening, he looked tired and … bored. He asked how we were doing, although it was probably a formality. Ultimately, he brought us one anti-tank disc mine. That's all we could afford.[53]

Around 0100 hours on 5 March, *Waffen-Oberführer* Puaud left his men for unknown reasons, the group being commanded in his absence by *Waffen-Hauptsturmführer* de Bourmont. Together with *Waffen-Sturmbannführer* de Vaugelas, *Waffen-Hauptsturmführer* Renault and *Waffen-Untersturmführer* Delil as a driver, Puaud set off in a *Volkswagen Type 82 Kübelwagen* in pursuit of the division's spearhead. Their journey came to an abrujpt end on the exit road from Karlino when the vehicle, in the dark, hit a wreck left on the highway. Uninjured, all of the group returned to the city on foot.[54]

The actual evacuation of the *Régiment de Réserve* began early on the morning of 6 March. After ordering *Waffen-Hauptsturmführer* Basompierre's rearguard to wait not 24, but 48 hours, most of the regiment – very poorly armed or even unarmed, with no grenadiers at all – and a number of civilians set off towards Białogard. At around 0800 hours, the column encountered a Soviet motorized unit. Panic crept into the French ranks. Many wanted to return to their starting point, while others were afraid,

52   F. Steiner, *Ochotnicy Waffen-SS…*, p. 230.
53   Memoirs of *Waffen-Untersturmführer* Michel de Genouillac, typescript in the author's collection. Robert Forbes recalls that Edgar Puaud also brought his subordinates smoked salmon, which after the hunger plaguing them for several days was a real treat. R. Forbes, *For Europe …*, p. 314. Another account mentions herrings, but given the abundance of salmon and sea trout in Parsęta, the previous version seems more likely.
54   J. Mabire, *La Division…*, p. 453.

looking for a wood in which to hide.[55] Despite the fact that the first Russians they encountered did not seem to notice the refugees, or took them for civilians, about half an hour later, when the fog cleared, a massacre occurred on the vast plain.

The regiment's annhilation began under violent fire from the enemy, shooting from the road leading towards Białogard. One unnamed survivor of these dramatic events recollected:

> About three thousand people this winter morning found themselves in a pine forest near Białogard. Tired, they moved about fifteen metres. Suddenly the sun came out and the fine rain stopped. The shooting started. The Russians were already here. Soldiers caught in the crossfire fell to the ground or tried to flee in any direction. The officers failed to control the group. The Russians shot them quickly. We were crushed by [fire from] rifles, machine guns, light cannons, and mortars. Pieces of soil and snow were rising around [us]. We were too tired to run and too nervous to hide. We walked around, still shooting. Finally we got to the forest. I looked back. There were Soviet soldiers and tanks on the plain. They killed our wounded.

Individual French platoons tried to escape. Further details of the day's events come from several accounts collected by Robert Forbes long after the end of the war, including one by *Waffen-Rottenführer* Sepchant:

> At dawn it turned out that we were in contact with the enemy. Shortly afterwards an officer on a horse passed us, shouting: 'Everyone to the north!' Instead, we headed south-east, straight into the mouth of the Soviet lion. In the confusion I noticed the NCO, who was probably out of his mind ... Nearby, sitting on the ground, a major was relaxing. When asked if he intended to go further, he replied apathetically: 'I am a doctor.' Shortly afterwards a Soviet tank drove nearby. I saw a ditch full of water, I decided to hide in it, immersed literally to the hole in the nose. Freezing, I heard the sounds of the ongoing fight. I cried. When there was silence, I left the ditch and wanted to move on alone. Suddenly, behind me, a Soviet patrol [rose] out of the under[growth]: two soldiers and a boy of twelve. They led me before an officer who interrogated me, fluent in German.

Waffen-Unterscharführer Mercier also remembered the one-sided confrontation with the Russians:

> We heard a cannonade on our right flank. Together with Captain Schliser, we saw a group of Soviet tanks launching an attack. We didn't have any anti-tank

---

55 R. Landwehr, *French Volunteers...*, p. 68.

weapons, so all we could do was hide in the bushes and wait for things to happen. We were hoping that the Russians would pass and we could continue the evacuation. There was growing panic. Schlisler tried to control us, silencing someone from time to time. Lieutenant Darrigade's platoon left the group, [and] decided to push through the forest on their own. We [saw] from a distance how some of our comrades in arms were killed or taken prisoner. The Russians also tried to penetrate the nearby forest, but fortunately it turned out to be too dense. Literally two steps away from me, one of the soldiers we called Roche committed suicide by shooting himself in the mouth with a Mauser rifle. I've known him since 1941. He served in the third company of the first battalion of the Legion of French Volunteers against Bolshevism. He was probably a driver at the current *Waffen-Sturmmann* level. He was rather controlled, he was rarely carried away. He used to say, 'Oh, it's like always.' I don't know how [long] we sat in the bushes. At one point, a fifteen-year-old Russian entered the brush. He was alone [amongst] our group, but he didn't notice anyone. I even thought about shooting him, but the rifle got stuck. Today I know that it may have [been fortunate], because the bang would certainly have attracted the attention of other Soviet soldiers. They were close … A moment later, the enemy was heading towards our safehouse. There was nothing else but to run blindly, through the open. At some point, we fell straight on the enemy tanks. Captain Schlisler decided to surrender the unit. Being powerless, he threw his submachine gun on the ground. I thought that in a moment I would end my life with a bullet in the back of the head. Instead, the Russians robbed us of our wrist watches.

Most men of the *Régiment de Reserve* destroyed their documents, fearing Soviet revenge. They fled in every direction, including towards the nearby massacre at Łęczynko (Lenzen-Vorwek) and Łęczno (Lenzen). Many of them fell into the hands of Russians located in nearby villages. Others, for example, *Waffen-Haupsturmführer* Bonnefoy – serving as a doctor – witnessed the immediate, brutal trials that Soviet soldiers conducted against their former comrades from the Russian Liberation Army in the vicinity of Białogard.[56]

It is now known that several dozen soldiers of the Reserve Regiment fled south, reaching Byszyno (Boissin) and Czarnowęsy (Zarnefanz), passing through Kamosowo and Gruszewo (Grüssow). They wandered around until the end of April, reaching either the Baltic or the Oder River basin. Their fate most often ended in Soviet or Polish captivity. *Waffen-Untersturmführer* Michel de Genouillac and *Waffen-Oberjunker* Andre Bayle were captured by soldiers of the 1st Polish Army. De Genouillac, together with several of his comrades, was taken prisoner on 15 March while heading for the Oder, and then, after a few weeks in a POW camp in Poznań, was handed over to the French authorities. In 1946, he was charged with collaboration. Bayle, a participant in

---

56   R. Forbes, *For Europe…*, pp. 320–25.

the Berlin Olympic Games in 1936, who previously commanded one of the platoons of the 2nd Company of the 1st Battalion of the *57. Waffen-Grenadier Regiment der SS*, was captured by Poles 10 days earlier and released to the Red Army. After the end of the war, he participated in a march of prisoners through the streets of Moscow, finally reaching a labour camp at Tambov on the Cna River, where many soldiers of the *33. Waffen-Grenadier Division der SS Charlemagne* were sent.

A description of the breakdown of the Reserve Regiment can be found in a monograph on the battles for Kołobrzeg by Alojzy Sroga. Due to the fact that it was the first account of the event, although probably based solely on indirect information collected by the Soviets, it is here quoted it in its entirety, in its original wording:

> The main forces of the French fascists with the French commander, general Puaud, numbering about three thousand people, are trying to approach Białogard. The commander is wounded. The fire of Soviet machine guns and artillery pushes armoured grenadiers[57] south-west from the city. At dawn they gathered in Czarnowęsy,[58] Rzyszczewo and Byszyno village. The forest there seems for them a safe place for a rest. To reach the forests, they must run through a great empty ground. They move. The giant fire of tank guns and 120mm mortars is falling from almost all sides. The division is massacred. Only a few manage to get to the forest. Most go to Soviet or Polish captivity. At 14.00 General Puaud was hobbled and leaning on a soldier on a wooden litter. And this was the last news about him. The Division's reserve subunits survived. One of them is a group of one hundred under the French marshal de Bourmont. They leave in a snowstorm. This is the last that is known of the men under de Bourmont.[59]

To this day, it has not been possible to determine the exact place where the Reserve Regiment was broken up. There is no doubt that it took place in the area between Redlino, Trzebielami and Rościn (Rostin), most likely in the bend on the right bank of the Parsęta. Although this area was scanned several times between 2000 and 2016, nothing conclusive was found.

The fate of *Waffen-Oberführer* Edgar Puaud is a separate issue, awakening the imagination of historians and military enthusiasts. According to information contained in a book by the commander of the *III (germanisches) SS-Panzerkorps*, *SS-Obergruppenführer* Felix Steiner, the French general was killed during Soviet shelling.[60] Richard Landwehr has suggested he was wounded and then evacuated

---

57   In fact the French Division were not a *Panzer-Grenadier* unit, as the author has stated.
58   The actual name is Czarnowęsy (Zarnefanz).
59   Description is of *Waffen-Hauptsturmführer* Victor de Bourmont. A. Sroga, *Na drodze…*, pp. 53–55.
60   F. Steiner, *Ochotnicy Waffen-SS…*, p. 229.

from the battlefield by one of the divisional car drivers.[61] This version seems to be confirmed by the previously quoted *Waffen-Untersturmführer* Michel de Genouillac, who claimed that Puaud, accompanied by *Waffen-Sturmbannführer* de Vaugelas, *Waffen-Hauptsturmführer* Renault and *Waffen-Untersturmführer* Delile, went to one of the German-held farms.[62]

Another version of the event was given by *Waffen-Obersturmführer* Multrier, referring to the story of a witness, an anonymous non-commissioned officer and former Vichy militiaman. He claimed that the wounded general was, along with others, evacuated by motorcycle to Gryfice. There, Puaud was left alone in one of the inns, then captured by Soviet soldiers (his companion was out looking for civilian clothing to help with their further escape). Other veterans of the *33. Waffen-Grenadier Division der SS Charlemagne* maintained that their commander had secretly survived the fall of the Third Reich and was later seen on the streets of Paris. The most unbelievable account concerns the alleged appearance of Egar Puaud as an *NKVD* officer in East Berlin. It is likely, however, that Puaud failed to escape with his life and, together with many of his comrades-in-arms, was buried in one of several mass graves that are still waiting to be located in the Białogard area.[63]

The remnants of 2nd Company of 1st Battalion avoided the destruction of the *Régiment de Reserve*, re-forming in Piotrowice under *Waffen-Obersturmführer* Bartolomei. The group, between 90 and 200 strong, served as a rearguard during a march on 6 March. The troops stopped about 2km from Karlino, waiting for orders that never came. When the morning fog rose, the officer decided to lead the group himself, avoiding contact with the enemy. They passed a Soviet column heading towards the city they had been defending a few hours earlier, probably in the footsteps of the 1st Battalion of the March Regiment. The company crossed the Parsęta on the northwestern edge of Białogard and hid in the surrounding forests. Around noon, about 100 French survivors from the massacre joined them, led by *Waffen-Hauptsturmführer* de Bourmont (this remains the last known trace of this officer). At around 0500 hours on 7 March, *Waffen-Untersturmführer* Rigeade's detachment – about 50 men – joined the group. The next day, the grenadiers encamped at an unknown farm on the trail leading to Gryfice, where they were surprised by a Russian unit. It was suspected that the Soviet soldiers had been alerted to their presence by a

---

61 R. Landwehr, *French Volunteers...*, p. 68.
62 A few days later, *Waffen-Sturmbannführer* Jean de Vaugelas was captured by Polish soldiers near Gryfice. During his interrogation, he minutely described the divisional organization and its history. A. Sroga, *Na drodze...*, p. 462.
63 In 2011, an attempt was made to find a grave in which, according to witnesses, up to 100 soldiers of the *33. Waffen-Grenadier Division der SS* were buried. It was allegedly located on the edge of the cemetery at Kołobrzeska Street in Białogard. However, it could not be located. J. Roszkowski, *Mogiła niemieckich żołnierzy w Białogardzie wciąż ukryta*, [w:] 'Głos Koszaliński', 12 October 2011.

Ukrainian forced labourer. The French were robbed of personal property, in particular rings and watches, and then taken into captivity.[64]

The division rearguard was now under the command of the current head of the 2nd Battalion of the Marching Regiment, *Waffen-Hauptsturmführer* Jean Basompierre. Before the French could retreat, they had to man the positions previously abandoned by their comrades from other units for several hours. Although the Red Army's numerical superiority was constantly increasing, the men of an experienced officer managed to destroy two Soviet tanks on the city's roads and repel several infantry attacks. In the sector manned by the remnants of the 1st Company, led by 23-year-old *Waffen-Hauptscharführer* Eric Walter, the French even carried out a brief counterattack. However, the group paid a heavy price, with the loss of more than half of their original complement – out of 750 grenadiers, only about 350 were later able to evacuate their positions.[65] The enemy employed megaphones in the area, broadcasting at regular intervals the message: "Frenchmen, give up. Join your Soviet comrades. You will return to France. You will not be treated like German *SS*-men, you are allies."[66]

The decision to break out was made during a meeting of the 2nd Battalion's staff on the night of 5–6 March. To minimize losses, the retreat was to be carried out by troops no more than a team in size, led by experienced non-commissioned officers, most likely veterans of the LVF and the French *SS*-Assault Brigade. The destination of the evacuation, which was to start between 0200 and 0300 hours the next night, was the Oder River basin, because it was rightly believed that the Baltic ports enabling escape to the west by sea were already in enemy hands. A transition to the vicinity of Białogard was initially planned, from where the group was to move northwest, towards Gryfice and beyond.[67]

The unit concentrated for the march at the railway station, where all remaining members of the *33. Waffen-Grenadier Division der SS Charlemagne* in Karlino arrived just after dark on 7 March. The role of rearguard was assigned to the 1st Company platoon commanded by *Waffen-Oberscharführer* Blaise. It was to periodically simulate combat by firing several volleys of automatic weapons or single shots in the air. This ploy aimed to mislead the Russians into believing that the defence of the city at the fork of the Parsęta and Radwia was continuing.

Waffen-Hauptsturmführer Basompierre's group set off in full moonlight, in teams of less than 10. Having crossed Koszalińska Street, the grenadiers arrived at the railway viaduct towering over the Radwia valley, which they crossed in pairs or threes. Passing through the forest on the east bank of the river, the group became embroiled in a fight with a strong Soviet patrol. In the glow of flares and exploding mortar grenades, the

---

64 R. Forbes, *For Europe...*, pp. 330–32.
65 It should be assumed that the remaining injured were too badly wounded to move on their own, or – which became typical at this stage of the *33. Waffen-Grenadier Division der SS* – escaped from Karlino.
66 Ch. de La Mazière, *Marzyciel w...*, p. 87.
67 R. Landwehr, *French Volunteers...*, p. 48.

Karlino railway station during the interwar period. From here, on 7 March 1945, a group of
French grenadiers commanded by *Waffen-Hauptsturmführer* Jean Basompierre – the last unit
of the *33. Waffen-Grenadier Division der SS Charlemagne* defending the fork of the Parsęta
and Radia rivers – began to break out of the city. (Studio Historycznego Huzar Archive)

Railroad tracks from Karlino (Körlin) on the viaduct over the Radwia towards Białogard
(Belgard an der Persante) in March 2017. This road, after dark on 7 March 1945, was chosen
by the last group of soldiers of the *Charlemagne* Division evacuating the city, commanded by
Waffen-Hauptsturmführer Jean Basompierre. (Photo Łukasz Gładysiak)

unit dispersed. The 30-strong rearguard platoon was the first to break contact, moving off on their own (eventually, on 18 April, five surviving men of Blaise's unit were captured by the Russians on the Oder). A staff section with a column commander fled northwards. A few hours later, they set off along the Parsęta on a hastily built raft.[68]

The core of the group managed to escape the chasing enemy and the eastern side of Białogard. After liquidating a Soviet post at one of the crossings over the Parsęta, a review of the retreat was ordered, which took place in a forest outside the city. One of the 300 Frenchmen present there, Christian La Mazière, recalled the event:

> The face of the individuals changed beyond recognition. Jean Basompierre was the only recognized commander [at that time]. Behind him [was] a natural hierarchy that had nothing to do with the regulatory structure. The column broke up into groups where the command was taken over by people with the strongest personality, the greatest endurance, with experience allowing [them] to take responsibility for human life on their shoulders.

Several hours' rest in the forest was interrupted by a sudden Soviet attack. On 8 March, the group managed to break away from the enemy and head northwest, towards the region's largest highway, today's National Road 6, probably passing the villages of Żabiniec (Wiesenhof), Kamosowo and Rościn. Awaiting the right moment to cross the trail full of enemy military vehicles, the French eventually had to give in to Soviet superiority on the morning of 9 March in the area around Kozia Góra (Koseeger). The breakup of the column initiated the tracking of the positions of the *33. Waffen Grenadier Division der SS Charlemagne* by the crew of one of the Soviet tanks. Seeing the tank's turret revolving, Walzer, armed with a *Panzerfaust* grenade launcher, fired and destroyed the armoured vehicle. Shortly after, the non-commissioned officer was fatally shot by a machine-gun burst. A moment later, two more Soviet tanks burst into flames. The Russians fired rapidly, trying to control the situation in an action that lasted between 15 minutes and half an hour. Flares illuminated an area of around a kilometre. "We shot everything that moved and looked like an enemy," Christian La Mazière recalled. "During the melee, which was the final [act] of the clash, [up to] a hundred Frenchmen [fled], among them the [remnants] of the subordinates of *Waffen-Haupsturmführer* Emile Monneuse."[69]

Those who managed to avoid being captured wandered the area around Białogard, Gryfice, Kołobrzeg and Świdwin for several consecutive days, eventually losing hope of joining any German units. Some arrived near Wolin (Wollin). An eloquent description of this exodus was included in the memoirs of a soldier of the 4th Company of the 2nd Battalion of the *Régiment de Marche*, Robert Lacoste:

68 R. Forbes, *For Europe...*, pp. 336–38.
69 R. Forbes, *For Europe...*, p. 341.

We walked along the edge of the forest. *Waffen-Obersturmführer* Jean Français [the company commander] checked the column from time to time, ensuring that no one was left behind. At one point a shot was fired. The bullet of the Soviet sniper shot him in the back. I hurried to help but he was already dead. I tore his dog tag, took the gun. There was no time for burial in the frozen ground. We had to leave the body on the path.[70]

A group led by *Waffen-Oberscharführer* Blonet, the core of which were the grenadiers of the battalion's 2nd Company and a unit of Latvians from the *15. SS-Grenadier Division*, decided to march only at night. On 17 March, near Sławoborze, the soldiers encountered a unit of the 1st Polish Army. The NCO commanding the group recalled:

In the morning, suffering from footbite comparable to that I had in 1941 near Moscow, I could no longer go on. I asked *Waffen-Oberscharführer* Veyrieras to take over the command of our group. His first decision, which I did not want to comment on, was to leave the forest that had been sheltering us for a long time, into an open space, during the day. They entered directly on a column of Poles and were immediately disarmed. In fact, this event probably saved my life. Comrades have informed me that I was wounded in the forest. A Polish military doctor, a Jew, helped load me onto a cart pulled by German prisoners of war. He fluently informed me in French that his regiment was composed mainly of soldiers who had previously been imprisoned by the Russians in Siberia in connection with the deportations of 1939–1940. He enlisted in the ranks of our enemy, wanting to return to his homeland. I was directed to Gryfice, and from there to a field hospital in Puławy. There, a German doctor amputated the frostbitten toes of my left foot.[71]

Basompierre did not escape captivity. He was captured by Polish soldiers on 17 March in the Karlino area, and shortly after the end of the war was deported to France. He managed to escape from prison but was arrested again on 28 October 1945 while trying to board a ship heading to Argentina. On 17 January 1948, he was sentenced to death for treason. The sentence was carried out on 20 April that year in the La Santé prison in Paris.

The only group members who managed to actually cross the Oder were *Waffen-Obersturmführer* de Bregeot's band of 20 or 30 troops. His actions came to an end only on 2 May on the Spree River in a confrontation with the Polish 1st Warsaw Cavalry Brigade. This meant that de Bregeot's unit covered a distance of nearly 250km, moving all the time over territory occupied by the enemy.[72]

---

70   Ibid., p. 338.
71   The majority of *Waffen-Oberscharführer* Blonet's unit were sent to Gryfice.
72   Ibid., pp. 345-46.

As calculated by Richard Landwehr, the total losses suffered by the *33. Waffen-Grenadier Division der SS Charlemagne* during the fighting around Karlino and Białogard, as well as the chaotic retreat of individual sub-units until the end of March 1945, could reach some 4,800 dead, wounded, missing and taken prisoners. As in the case of the fighting in the vicinity of Czarne, this number is still difficult to confirm or reject. What is certain is that, less than two weeks after arriving at the front at Wildflecken and Gryfice, the French division was virtually completely broken up. From the end of the first week of March 1945, it no longer represented any combat value as a compact unit. In combat, not only was virtually 100 percent of its machinery lost, including almost all of the artillery, but also a significant number of small arms and manual anti-tank weapons, not counting the elements of uniforms, commonly exchanged at the time for civilian clothes, or combat equipment, which can still be found in the area to this day. Any further activities of *SS-Brigadeführer* Gustav Krukenberg's group were undertaken as several battle groups that were part of other larger, most often improvised units. Total defeat in the Pomeranian campaign was now only a matter of time.

5

Back to the Baltic

The first three months of 1945 was a critical period for *Reichsführer-SS* Heinrich Himmler's . On 24 February, the Red Army – acompanied by 1st Polish Army – launched the Pomeranian operation, which through concentric attacks by units of the 1st and 2nd Belorussian Fronts was to eliminate the salient created in the area of the *Wehrmacht Wehrkreis II* (Military District Number 2) still controlled by German forces. After two days of action, the Russians entered Biały Bór (Baldenburg) and approached Szczecinek and Bobolice. On 3 March, Świdwin was in Soviet hands, and after the capture of Polanów (Pollnow) the spearhead of the Soviet 3rd Tank Corps was near Koszalin. The same day, Soviet forces stood on the shores of the Baltic Sea, in the town of Łazy. Twenty-four hours later, the 45th Guards Tank Brigade boldly hit north and reached the first of the three defensive lines at Kolobrzeg, starting a siege lasting two weeks (from 6 March, the burden of capturing *Festung Kolberg* rested on the Poles and the combat group led by General Marek Karakoz, frontline deputy commander of the 1st Polish Army). The day before, in Mrzeżyno (Treptower Deep), 10km north of Trzebiatów, the forces of General Mikhail Katukov reached the Baltic shore, confirming this fact by drawing its water in their field flasks, while the Soviet 3rd Shock Army attacked Nowogard (Naugard). Just a few hours earlier, the remains of German garrisons at Pyrzyce and Stargard had capitulated. Most of the units in the X SS-Armeekorps enclosed in the Schivelbein Pocket were also forced to lay down their arms.

The rapid progress of the invaders meant that most German units in Pomerania were pushed to the coast. They all suffered shortages in group and individual armament, ammunition and equipment. Supplies of winter uniforms did not reach many units, which further reduced the low morale of the soldiers. There was also a shortage of food and drinking water. Chaos during the retreats was intensified by crowds of civilian fugitives trying to escape the inevitable revenge of the Soviets at all costs. There was also virtually no local administration.[1]

---

1 In addition to the movement of columns of German refugees hindering the march of

A column of 1st Polish Army vehicles on their way to Kołobrzeg (Kolberg) in the first days of its siege. The photo was taken at the Trzebiatów (Treptow an der Rega) and Świdwin (Schivelbein) crossroads. It was here that *Waffen-Rottenführer* Robert Soulat from the *Charlemagne* headquarters company managed to reach on the night of 3/4 March 1945 just after the French–Soviet clash in Gościno (Gross Jestin). (Museum of the Polish Arms Archive)

It should be assumed that the staff of the *Charlemagne* Division, or rather what remained of it after the devastating battle around Karlino and Białogard, did not know about most of these problems. Soldiers scattered throughout almost the entire eastern part of *Provinz Pommern*, holding positions that were shrinking hour by hour, independently tried to break through in the direction of the Oder or, which was particularly the case for companies traversing Central Pomerania, to the Baltic. Some placed their hope in connection with the larger formations of the Third Reich and the opportunity to participate in a better-organized retreat to the west. Others believed that being in one of the Baltic ports would make it possible to flee to Bornholm Island, Jutland and even to neutral Sweden.

the troops, also destructively affecting the morale of *Wehrmacht* soldiers was the attitude of civilians escaping from the territories occupied by the Red Army, who told of their traumatic experiences. One of the most vivid such descriptions is contained in a book entitled *Wielka Ucieczka* by Jürgen Thorwald (Polish issue, Warsaw: 2009).

Whilst Białogard was being defended, a separate group of Frenchmen found themselves in the area of today's Kołobrzeg. In the first days of March, Gościno, located about 20km from the Baltic,[2] had been reached by soldiers deployed from Gryfice, including the engineer sub-units and HQ elements. These were led by *Waffen-Sturmbannführer* Katzian. One of the forced labourers and Polish pioneers, Tadeusz Opiela, saw the French SS-grenadiers, as related by Alojzy Sroga: "A group of seriously frightened French SS men from the *Charlemagne* Grenadier Division stopped for a long time in the centre of Gościna Tatra in a truck with a wood gas engine. The officer, unshaven like his soldiers, and fatally tired, drew out a map. Just in case, he asked passers-by: 'is this really Gościno?' … He tilts his head so as not to hear the louder and louder French and German curses on the platform behind him."[3] Opiela also mentioned that when the sign sewn on his clothes with the letter 'P' was spotted, which all Polish forces workers in the Third Reich were obliged to wear, the commanding officer informed him that the Polish Army which he and his men had recently fought was approaching Gościno.[4]

Some French, during the fight for Karlino, were heading northwest. Among them was *Waffen-Rottenführer* Robert Soulat, who observed:

On Sunday, March 4, 1945, along the road through Kowanz and Kerstin I reached the town of Gross Jestin with a veteran of the Volunteers Legion responsible for the forage to the animals remaining in our division. [He was LVF member] *Waffen-Unterscharführer* Favreau. The town seemed quite large to me, I counted about 200 people in uniforms, of course mainly German. Knowing that the core of our division gathered several kilometres south of Körlin, we tried to organize those who had not participated in the fights so far. There was a lot to choose from, not only members of the staff company gathered in the town, but also field gendarmerie, divisional writers, soldiers responsible for the field post office, and finally Germans from the well-known division inspectorate. We had four or five trucks [and probably one *Volkswagen Type 82 Kübelwagen*]. Finally, 80 of us were ready to fight.

Although *Waffen-Hauptscharführer* Augustin, who organized a briefing, informed us that we were safe, we had to be ready to fill the so-called third line of defence. In addition, he warned us of the risk of, for example, enemy paratroopers. Few of us knew what it meant. We came to the conclusion that this 'security' should be looked at with a grain of salt. Finally, we were divided into two platoons. One of them was to immediately – around 2200 hours – set off to the outposts, i.e. the area leading from the city in a southerly direction

---

2   In 1945, Gościno, which has been a town since 2011, was a large village on the road from Świdwin to Kołobrzeg.
3   A. Sroga, *Na drodze…*, pp. 33-34.
4   *Noce i dnie… Ocalić od zapomnienia*, Gościno BDW, p. 5.

and become an 'alarm guard'. I was in the 2nd Platoon. At about 0200 we were supposed to relieve our comrades."[5].

The 1st Platoon was commanded by *Waffen-Oberscharführer* Lallemand, an LVF veteran who had previously been responsible for the divisional station *Feldpost*. The place of lodging for the others was the school building (now a residential building) at today's Tadeusz Kościuszko Street. The road to Gościn, regardless of the route chosen, was not safe – most of the roads were controlled by either soldiers of the Red Army or local militia units formed spontaneously, mainly by forced labourers brought to the region, mostly Poles. The militia abducted *Waffen-Obersturmführer* Bénétoux, responsible for the division machinery park, and handed over to Soviet officers. After a short interrogation, he joined a column of prisoners, but managed to escape and reach German lines.[6] In all, about 80 French SS-men were gathered together.[7]

The reorganization of the *33. Waffen-Grenadier Division der SS Charlemagne* in Gościn came to an end on the night of 3/4 March. At the same time, the spearhead of the

Waffen-Rottenführer Robert Soulat (here in the rank of *Waffen-Sturmmann*), a member of the headquarters (staff) company of *33. Waffen-Grenadier Division der SS Charlemagne*. This photograph was taken at Wildflecken in September 1944. (Studio Historyczne Huzar Archive)

Soviet 45th Guards Tank Brigade appeared in the village, heading in the direction of Kołobrzeg. The Soviets did not expect any resistance, but despite being surprised by the presence of the enemy, *Waffen-Sturmbannführer* Katzian's grenadiers put up

5   Robert Soulat's letter to author, preserved in his private archive.
6   R. Forbes, *For Europe…*, p. 307. This author mentions that in the column led by *Waffen-Obersturmführer* Bénétoux there were also French forced labourers and citizens of the Third Republic freed from nearby prisoner of war camps who had been captured by the Germans during the 1940 campaign. The latter were indignant to be included in the group of collaborators.
7   *Waffen-Rottenführer* Robert Soulat memoirs…, p. 26.

a fight. The night-time skirmish, which was later described by *Waffen-Rottenführer* Soulat, took place on the southern edge of today's IV Dywizji Wojska Polskiego Street:

> Around 1.30 am we were woken up to take over the guard at the station. It seemed that nothing special had happened so far and peace was all around. We were preparing to leave. We left the school and soon turned left into the main street of Gościno clogged with various vehicles and a crowd of refugees. We set off on the right side to the south, towards the edge of the village. The road was like a ditch, that is, a pit between two high embankments. We jumped to the edge of the ditch and in twos, with a weapon on our shoulder, we moved further along the edge.
>
> Suddenly, at the head of our column, one of the companions shouted: 'Hey, guys, look, Russian captives are coming!' Immediately afterwards a second voice said: '"No, they are armed!' Then there was an incredible scene, lasting only a few seconds; the first rows of both columns – French and Russian – faced each other and ... raised their hands up! Behind us, our men started shouting gutturally: 'Shit, fuck! Shoot, don't stand!' You could also hear the screams of Russians, probably [with a] similar content. The tail of our column shattered: the soldiers ran towards the wall of a house standing nearby and began to climb the fence. Some took positions. Only then did the shooting break out. Three or four Frenchmen, including me, ran away from the road. We threw ourselves into the ground, taking positions. Under fire, however, some of the soldiers decided to take up alternative positions with the possibility of escaping if the Soviets broke through. It also seemed that some tanks were following the Russian lead, which, in order to clear the route, fired a few shots on the axis of the road. Missiles exploded between the crowded refugees.

Later it became clear that *Waffen-Oberscharführer* Lallemand's platoon was guilty of not recognizing that the Soviets were arriving, as Soulat continued:

> According to their accounts, they took a fixed 'alarm position' and conscientiously served guard. At one point they noticed the silhouettes of three tanks emerging in the dark, but they had not seen any retreating German troops, and on one of the tanks someone was sitting whistling and playing a harmonica; laughter was also heard. It seemed to them that it could not be an enemy. Of course, as soon as they realized the mistake, they withdrew as quietly as possible, taking the shortest route, probably through nearby allotments. Resistance was pointless in this case – the platoon did not have a single *Panzerfaust*, all were given to the Marching Regiment left in Körlin. Hand-firing at tanks was pointless. However, if we had any anti-tank weapons, it would be only a matter of time before the destruction of these machines – they probably stopped due to lack of

fuel, and the positions of the first platoon were located on a hill, slightly above [where] the Russian stopped.[8]

Around 0200 hours on 4 March, a decision was made, due to the evident threat from the Red Army and the lack of resources to put up any real resistance, to evacuate from Gościn to a little over 30km northwest of Trzebiatów. Around 0330 hours, the last evacuation train with civilians left Kołobrzeg.[9] Troops began a feverish search for means of transport, realizing that covering such a large distance on foot in completely unknown terrain, and alone, may prove impossible. Several trucks were used for the transfer, and the column was completed by a *Volkswagen*-type *Kübelwagen* driven by *Waffen-Obersturmführer* Meier.[10]

Not everyone managed to leave the town, and some were left to their own devices. Among them was *Waffen-Rottenführer* Soulat, who, after the clash with Soviet tanks, did not return to the school building, but moving probably via today's Adama Mickiewicz Street, he walked around the western edge of Gościno along present day Towarowa Street. Ten kilometres to the north, he finally reached the intersection of Provincial Road 162 with the road leading to Rościęcino (Rossenthin), only 8km from the centre of Kołobrzeg. There he was arrested by a patrol of German *Feldgendarmerie*, as he later related:

> From nowhere, I come across a blockade of four or five 'chained cows', as we called German gendarmes because of the gorgets hung on chains. Their vehicles were parked right next to the road. They stopped me and told me to turn left onto the road leading to Trzebiatów. Nobody could get to Kołobrzeg at that time. During the conversation, I noticed a *Wehrmacht* company-size unit armed with two 80mm mortars, which occupied positions on the farm located on the left side of the road. The barrels turned south. I also saw streaks of illuminating flares that ended their flight, landing about one and a half, maybe two kilometers from us. I entrusted the gendarmes and decided to actually move in the direction indicated.[11]

Gościno was seized by the Red Army at around 0500 hours on 4 March by elements of the Soviet 45th Guards Tank Brigade.[12] Soulat reached Wolin through Trzebiatów, and then used the ferry crossing to the island of Usedom. The column of *Charlemagne*

---

8 Robert Soulat's letter sent to author on 22 March 2012 preserved in author's archive.
9 *Noce i dnie...*, p. 5.
10 In the letter quoted above, Robert Soulat mentions that among the French grenadiers there was also an armed civilian, most likely a worker. During one of the stops he tried to shoot several soldiers, but was quickly rendered harmless.
11 *Waffen-Rottenführer* Robert Soluat memoirs..., p. 28.
12 The Red Army units departed almost immediately towards Kołobrzeg, handing over the town to the control of the Polish Army. On 7 March, soldiers of the Polish 3rd Infantry

vehicles reached Wolin, then on 5 March, around 0600 hours, set off via Kamień Pomorski (Kammin) to Świnoujście (Swinemünde), which they reached the next day. On 7 March, a group of 200 was evacuated 50km west to the Mecklenburg town of Jargelin near Anklam. They consisted not only of soldiers leaving various parts of Pomerania, but also some troops who had earlier disembarked at the railway station in Wolin. The soldiers, with neither weapons nor a large part of their combat equipment, arrived at Jargelin around 1600 hours. A week later, they were transferred to Menzlin on the Peene River. From there, they went to the place of the next reorganization of the division, in Neustrelitz.

A group of a dozen or so under the leadership of *Waffen-Untersturmführer* Sarrailhé are believed to have remained in *Festung Swinemünde*, taking part in its defence. The commander survived the battle, and in April he registered in Neustrelitz, later becoming the head of the 8th Company in the latest reorganization of the *58. Waffen-Grenadier Regiment der SS*. The fate of the soldiers of the other battalion, which during the Pomeranian campaign did not leave Gryfic, is a mystery. It cannot be discounted that they took part in brief battles with the Russians and elements of 1st Polish Army, which ended in the final capture of the city on 8 March.[13]

The next action seen by troops of the *33. Waffen-Grenadier Division der SS* during the Pomeranian campaign was the siege of *Festung Kolberg* by Soviet units and the 1st Polish Army. The decision that the largest port of Central Pomerania, as well as a number of other cities located in today's Poland – but then within greater Germany – would receive the fortress status was made on 28 November 1944. Soon after, the original plan of defending this symbolic city of Kolberg was outlined. It assumed the preparation of three defensive lines: two of them were to run 12km (outer ring) and 5km (inner ring) from the city, while the last one was based on its outskirts. *Generalmajor* Paul Hermann was appointed commander of the improvised garrison. As elsewhere in the Third Reich, units of national defence – the *Volkssturm* – were formed. They were gathered into a regiment group, led by a newcomer from Koszalin, *Marine-SA-Standartenführer* Erhard Pfeiffer. He was also entrusted with commanding the western defence section.

When the Gneisenau alarm was announced in the Second Military District on 20 January 1945, an alarm battalion was formed in Kołobrzeg, based on soldiers of the 4th Spare Grenadier Battalion Kolberg stationed here. To the surprise of the officers of the fortress staff, it was decided that this grouping would not remain at the mouth of the Parsęta. Most of the platoons were sent to Kostrzyn (Küstrin) on the Oder, and some went to Wismar in Mecklenburg. Six days after the announcement of the last mobilization for German Pomerania, the *Festung Kolberg* staff was formally

---

Division seized Gościno, along with Polish 4th Infantry Division sub-units. *Noce i dnie...*, p. 6.

13 R. Forbes, *For Europe...*, pp. 349–50.

established. A sapper colonel responsible for the technical side of the defence plan – Gerhard Troschel – also arrived.

Throughout February, soldiers were gathered in the city, creating various – often totally mixed – alarm sub-units. According to the calculations of the creator of the only publication so far presenting the whole battle from the German side, Johannes Volker, the garrison was to eventually comprise about 3,300 *Volkssturm* and regular soldiers. On 20 February, suffering from sciatica, Hermann was dismissed. His place was taken briefly by *Oberst* Gerhard Troschel. Eight days later, he was replaced by North African campaign veteran *Oberst* Fritz Fullriede, whose name is now indelibly connected with the two-week drama of *Festung Kolberg*.[14]

Despite the internal disagreements that sometimes turned into open personal conflicts, especially between professional army officers and prominent local NSDAP figures, a final plan for defending the fortress was created. With the leading Soviet forces already heading towards Białogard and Karlino, it was decided to shorten the three defensive lines and deploy positions based on the city limits. The whole was divided into three sections: the eastern (codenamed Leibjäger), which was manned for the most part by ground troops; the central (Indigo), defended by Kriegsmarine forces; and the western (Nußknacker), which was handed over to Volkssturm as well as Luftwaffe units.

In the testimonies of German troops who took part in the battle, there is often mention of the varied armaments which were issued from Kołobrzeg's military warehouses. In addition to the standard small arms used in the Third Reich, the front line was also issued with Italian and French rifles. The core of the anti-tank defence was manual weapons, primarily disposable *Panzerfaust* grenade launchers.[15] Several armoured vehicles (no less than seven, but no more than 18) were put at the disposal

14 As Johannes Volker points out, the decision to delegate this officer to the mouth of the Parsęta was dictated by his achievements on the North African front. In Berlin, the effort Fullriede put into the preparation and defence of the Pichon-Fondouk isthmus in Tunisia was still remembered. A combat group commanded by him based on elements of the 999. Infanterie-Division maintained their positions from 6–12 April 1943, despite overwhelming enemy forces. Opponents of the new commander – whose swearing-in, which is worth emphasizing, especially in the context of the subsequent arbitrary evacuation, never took place – reminded him of his repeated insubordination with his immediate superiors and the fact that he represented a party strongly associated with suicide of *Feldmarschall* Erwin Rommel after the assassination attempt of Adolf Hitler in July 1944. In addition, from the beginning of his stay in Kołobrzeg, Fritz Fullriede could not communicate with the city's civilian defence commandant, *Kreisleiter* Anton Gerriets. This resulted in the assignment to the staff of *Festung Kolberg* of a specific controller on behalf of the National Socialist German Workers' Party, *SS-Oberführer* Bertling.

15 The fact that there was no shortage of this type of weapon in Kołobrzeg at that time can be proved not only by accounts of German soldiers, but also by those of Poles. It was during the fighting near the mouth of the Parsęta that *Panzerfaust* grenade launchers were to be used for the first time by soldiers of the 1st Polish Army.

of the *Festung Kolberg* staff. They were collected into the hastily created *Panzergruppe Beyer*, which was commanded by *Leutnant* Eugena Beyer.[16]

By the time the German garrison of Kolobrzeg entered the final phase of preparations for the defence, the Soviet–Polish attack towards the mouth of the Parsęta was well underway. Their main axes ran through Słosinko (Reinfeld) near Miastko, Świdwin, Gościno and Połczyn Zdrój, Rąbino, Białogard and Karlino up to Rościęcinia, the village lying directly on the outskirts of *Festung Kolberg*. By 4 March, Soviet artillery was deployed in positions around the settlements of Bezpraw (Kautzenberg) and Rościęcino – on the edge of the Kołobrzeski forest – Mirocice (Bullenwinkel), Obroty (Wobrow) and Ustronie Morskie (Henkenhagen). No resistance was encountered in any of these places. The pace of the enemy's attack meant that the majority of the civilian population, despite evident signs of the upcoming battle, remained at home in accordance with the orders of the local NSDAP unit, waiting for an official evacuation order.

As recalled by a doctor in Kołobrzeg, Gerhard Haenisch, 4 March – the first day of the city's siege – began with extremely unfavorable weather conditions; freezing rain and snow fell, so most residents decided to remain at home instead of making use of the last chance of evacuation.[17] From 0100 hours, Fullriede suspended the operation of the civilian authorities. Placards were posted on walls declaring that almost a century and a half after its last siege, Kołobrzeg was again on the front line:

> The Soviets are approaching Kołobrzeg. A state of siege is being declared for the city and surrounding area. All power passes into the hands of the fortress commander. Acts of sabotage, robbery and any other act that weakens the *Wehrmacht* will be punished by immediate execution. Everyone in Kołobrzeg, but not yet scheduled soldiers of the *Wehrmacht*, with the exception of women's crews, cannot leave without a valid document issued by the city headquarters and should immediately report to the barracks.

The first Soviet units to enter the fight for *Festung Kolberg*, straight from the march, were the armoured vehicles of the 45th Guards Tank Brigade, which at arrived in the Neugeldern district (today's Radzikowo) at about 0430 hours, striking towards the city centre. Ninety minutes later, another group of vehicles reached the Karslberg brewery (Więcemino today), from where several tanks began to slowly move along Trzebiatowska Street. Early in the morning, the German defenders opened fire. It

---

16   Photographic evidence confirms the participation in the fighting of at least four *Jagdpanzer 38 (t) Hetzer* tank destroyers, which most probably came from *Panzer Division Holstein*, plus one *Pz.Kpfw. IV Ausf. H* medium tank and a single *Pz.Kpfw. III Ausf. E*. In addition, under the command of *Leutnant* Beyer but abandoned during the fighting was a half-track anti-aircraft self-propelled 3.7cm *Flak auf Sd.Kfz.*, i.e. *Sd.Kfz. 7/2* with an armoured cab variant.
17   J. Voelker, *Ostatnie dni…*, p. 46.

seemed to the Red Army staff that resistance in the city would last only for several hours, so a report was sent to the Moscow authorities stating that the largest port in Central Pomerania had been secured.

Around 1400 hours on 4 March, the Kolobrzeg turnpike was crossed by a group of soldiers of the 33rd SS-Artillery Squadron under the command of *Waffen-Hauptsturmführer* Jean Havette. Instead of its nominally assigned eight 105mm light field howitzers, which were being transported to the Baltic coast by rail, they were equipped with *Panzerfausts*.[18] In the first hours of the unit's presence in *Festung Kolberg*, *Waffen-Oberscharführer* Ranc destroyed one of the Soviet tracked armoured vehicles[19] (the location of this event has not been determined so far, but it probably took place on the southwestern edge of the city). On the same day, groups of Frenchmen from the area of Gościn and Dygowo (Degow) managed to enter the city. Alojzy Sroga, referring to the memories of soldiers of the Polish Army in the East, vividly described the state most of *SS-Brigadeführer* Krukenberg's men were in: "Bearded faces are overgrown, red, bad. Some have frostbitten hands or noses, others legs. Weapons [are] thrown down, rusted, not cleaned for weeks, [and there are] torn uniforms, shredded shoes." Apart from that, practically everyone suffered from hunger and they were extremely exhausted, from earlier fights and after a 30km march from Karlino.[20]

This signet ring, probably belonging to one of the soldiers of the *33. Waffen-Grenadier Division der SS Charlemagne*, was found on the route of the group's retreat from Karlino to Kołobrzeg. Engraved on the front is the unofficial emblem of the French division – a sword and oak leaves. (Maciej Cichecki Collection)

18   These 10.5cm *leichte Feldhaubitzen 18* were taken over by the staff of *Festung Kolberg* and most probably issued to sub-units of the ground forces. There was a rumour among the men of *Waffen-Hauptsturmführer* Havette about the delivery of new guns by sea.

19   R. Forbes, *For Europe...*, p. 312.

20   A. Sroga, *Na drodze...*, p. 54. Robert Forbes also confirms the dramatic condition and morale of the French *Waffen-SS* soldiers at that time.

Some 600 men of the *Charlemagne* Division joined the fight at Kołobrzeg. They were gathered in the area of the garrison casino located at today's Edmund Łopuski Street. As Robert Forbes has established, the command was originally intended to be entrusted to *Waffen-Hauptsturmführer* Havette or one of the group's most experienced officers, a 63-year-old veteran of the First World War, *Waffen-Obersturmführer* Multrier, but they were considered unsuitable due to their low morale.[21] Ultimately, the choice was made on 5 March of *SS-Obersturmführer* Ludwig, who came from the division staff and the ranks of the LVF. Swiss-born *SS-Untersturmführer* Heinrich Büller was appointed as his deputy.[22] Some 200 French fighters were gathered as part of the *Compagnie de Marche*; the remaining 400, who were previously disarmed, were sent to build fortifications and direct the movement of columns of civilian refugees. Among the commanders of platoons and teams of those assigned to fight was *Waffen-Oberjunker* Claude Platon, son of the minister for the colonies in the Vichy government, Admiral Rene-Charles Plato, who had been executed for treason on 28 August 1944. The *Compagnie de Marche* was included in *Alarmbataillon Hempel* under the command of *Reservieren Leutnant* Alfred Hempel.[23]

Ludwig's men joined the battle for the city on the morning of 6 March. *Alarmbataillon Hempel* counterattacked from the Drzewny Canal along Trzebiatowska Street. The target of the attack, supported by fire from the *Panzerzug 72A* armoured train operating around the railway station, were positions taken a few hours earlier by elements of the Soviet 362nd Self-propelled Artillery Regiment. Although the Soviets were thrown back, the German–French unit failed to break through towards Radzikowo, thwarted by the shelling of the area by 120mm mortar grenades and the introduction of Red Army sub-units equipped with flamethrowers. Also, not for the last time during the battle, vehicles with megaphones were brought to the front line by the Soviets, through which a teacher who spoke fluent German urged Hempel's men to desert.[24]

The following day, members of the *Charlemagne* Division encountered Polish soldiers for the first time during the fighting for Kołobrzeg. They were a group of prisoners captured most likely on the west bank of the Drzewny Canal and taken to the staff

---

21   R. Forbes, *For Europe...*, pp. 358–59.

22   L. Saint-Loup, *Les hérétiques...*, p. 301.

23   This unit, probably numbering about 400 soldiers of various formations, was established only a few hours before the beginning of the Soviet attack on the city. Like the vast majority of units in the garrison, it was deprived of heavy weapons, but well saturated with manual anti-tank weapons. Contrary to the opinion promoted by the historiography of the Polish People's Republic, *Alarmbataillon Hempel* was not a *Waffen-SS* unit, and its commander was not part of the *SS* officer corps. For commanding his improvised battlegroup during the defence of *Festung Kolberg*, *Leutnant* Hempel was awarded the Knight's Cross of the Iron Cross on 30 April 1945. He died in 1989. Ł. Gładysiak, *Batalion Alarmowy Hempel*, [w:] 'Głos Kołobrzegu', Friday 28 February 2014 (Koszalin: 2014), p. 5.

24   R. Landwehr, *French Volunteers...*, p. 76.

The courtyard of the garrison casino at today's Edmund Łopuski Street in Kołobrzeg after the fight for the city. From here, in the first days of March 1945, the soldiers of the *33. Waffen-Grenadier Division der SS Charlemagne* started fighting for the city. (Museum of Polish Arms Archives)

of the 3rd Infantry Division of Romuald Traugutt. Alojzy Sroga noted: "'Fantastic' testimonies were taken by the captured French *Panzer* Grenadiers from the 33rd *SS*-Division. Each of them emphasized that he was forcibly incorporated into this formation. Oh, he was at work in Germany, he got in touch with a German girl who became pregnant. An alternative remained: the concentration camp or 'voluntarily' join the 33rd *SS*-Division *Charlemagne*." However, a will was found on one of the captured Frenchmen, in which, citing the idea of the anti-Bolshevik crusade and the need to jointly defend European civilization against the invaders from the East, he explained his reasons for enlistment.[25]

On 8 March, *Festung Kolberg* was completely surrounded by Soviet and Polish forces. Probably unaware of this fact, two platoons of the *Compagnie de Marche* and several other teams of *Alarmbataillon Hempel* began another counterattack along Trzebiatowska Street at 0600 hours. His goal was to create a breach in the lines occupied by the Polish 18th Infantry Regiment, which would allow civilians

25   A. Sroga, *Na drodze…*, p. 59.

Today's Kamienna, Radomskiej, Trzebiatowska and Wolności Streets in Kołobrzeg (Kolberg) – the place of the debut in battle of the French *Compagnie de Marche* during the fighting in the city which took place on the morning of 6 March 1945. (Łukasz Gładysiak)

temporarily trapped in the vicinity of Radzikowo, Korzyścienko and Więcemino to get to the city centre and the harbour district. The French grenadiers reached the first of these areas after half an hour of tough fighting. It took them about five-and-a-half hours to get to the next one. Around 1700 hours, they managed to throw the enemy back to their starting positions in the Karlsberg heights. However, the Frenchmen had to retreat from the positions they has taken because the large open spaces provided no shelter in the event of artillery shelling.[26]

That same day, the attacking forces moved the focus of their activities from what is nowadays Trzebiatowska Street to Lęborskie Przedmieście, i.e. the area located near Grochowska and Koszalińska Streets, as well as National Road 11 and Kupiecka and Bogusława X Streets, including the area of the former Church of St George and the adjacent cemetery. The new main attack zone largely featured Polish sub-units in the Stramnica (Alt Tramm) and Niekanin (Necknin) area. Meanwhile, artillery fire

26   Ibid., pp. 102–12. The counterattack is confirmed by Louis Saint-Loup, Les hérétiques…, p. 306.

and air bombardments were intensified, which during this period were concentrated primarily on the densely built-up area of Śródmieście. The commander of *Festung Kolberg* said in the mid-1950s that every day between 1400 and 1900 hours, shells and grenades of various calibres hit the area in preparation for evening raids by units of infantry. Knowing that the Germans suffered from a lack of water, the Russians ensured that a significant percentage of the ammunition used were incendiary shells. Fires also spread due to gusty winds blowing from the Baltic Sea, which often reached severe gale force.[27]

SS-Obersturmführer Ludwig's troops were deployed to defend this section. Robert Forbes suggests that *Oberst* Fullriede ordered the French to maintain the intersection of today's Koszalińska, Jerzy, Myśliwska and Grochowska Streets and a rail crossing less than 1km to the east, which can currently be found on National Road 11 near the former Jewish cemetery.[28] After dark, members of the *Compagnie de Marche* quickly prepared defensive strongpoints in the houses' basements, with underground passages between the buildings having been earlier broken through.[29]

It must be assumed that at this time, the elements of the *33. Waffen-Grenadier Division der SS Charlemagne* were divided into at least two units, operating independently of each other. While some of them arrived at Lęborskie Przedmieście, others tried to defend the outposts around the training camp of the *Kriegsmarine* Torpedo School – the so-called Gneisenau Camp – and the anti-tank ditch in that part of the city. This area was the target of an enemy attack just after 1500 hours on 9 March.

That same day, a four-day battle for Lęborskie Przedmieście began. The aforementioned church of St George and the neighbouring cemetery became a German redoubt, with French fighters making a major contribution to their defence. Alojzy Sroga described the conditions under which they fought: "The cemetery complex is surrounded by a high wall, which was high enough to be a prison wall. It was unscrupulously included in the city's defence system. Every solid tree, every impressive tomb with a monument is a point of resistance; a stand for a heavy machine gun, concealment for a light tank or lurking 'tank destroyer' with an armoured fist."[30]

---

27   Ibid., p. 89.
28   Today, the described area differs significantly from the buildings existing in March 1945. The majority of tenement houses in Lęborski Przedmieście were destroyed, meaning the organization and purpose of the district were changed in the post-war period. Currently, the greater part of it is occupied by commercial and service facilities, including large stores and petrol stations. However, the location of the railroad crossing did not change.
29   R. Forbes, *For Europe...*, p. 360.
30   A. Sroga, *Na drodze...*, p. 192.

The former church of St George in Kołobrzeg, after being conquered by Polish Army forces. It was one of the places that soldiers of the *Charlemagne* Division defended during the battle for the city, but also a gathering point for those taken into into Polish captivity. (Museum of Polish Arms in Kołobrzeg Archives)

The fighting began here with the Poles attempting to break through the defensive belt between the gasworks and the edge of the district. The artillery observer Corporal Ernst Toews later recounted:

> Almost no people could be seen, only single soldiers could be seen on the street corners, with rifles on their shoulder ready to fire. They waited for the Russians leading the assault along the streets to come [the author incorrectly assessed the Germans' opponents in Lęborskie Przedmieście to be Russians; they were soldiers of the 1st Polish Army]. Single cows stood between the burning remains of the houses. They burned alive – they didn't take a single step to save themselves … Right behind the backyard gardens, in the meadows, there was Russian infantry [*sic*]. To the left of the observation point was the pointed tower of the small church of St George. There was an injured [man] in the corridor, blood spilled onto the tiles around him. He lay completely still on his back, then he died.[31]

On 10 March, the French carried out the first of a series of coordinated counterattacks against positions taken by soldiers of the 1st Battalion of the 7th Polish Infantry Regiment. The command post of *SS-Obersturmführer* Ludwig, who most likely did not take part in the fighting at that time, was in the apartment of one of the buildings at ul. Koszalińska. Probably wanting to discredit Ludwig, Alojzy Sroga noted in his writing on the battle for Kołobrzeg that the daughter of the property's owners was forced to serve the commander of the *Compagnie de Marche*, and was even supposed to give him breakfast in bed.[32] Although this passage should be considered fantasy, the author of the book confirms the location of Ludwig's headquarters. Furthermore, Louis Saint-Loup informs us that on this day, a four-man section appeared in the area of the *Compagnie de Marche* under the command of *Waffen-Sturmmann* Marotin from the *57. Waffen-Grenadier Regiment der SS*'s former 8th Company. Since losing contact with elements of their parent division in Szczecinek, they had fought in an improvised platoon created with men of the *4. SS-Polizei Division*, who for reasons not yet determined had reached Białogard.[33]

In order to oust the Poles from the walls of the cemetery, two combat groups were formed, led by NCOs selected from the ranks of the *Compagnie de Marche Waffen-Oberscharführer* Franc[34] and *Waffen-Unterscharführer* Ayme-Blot. In tough hand-to-hand fighting, both sides used not only the firearms but also bayonets and trench knives.[35] Temporarily regaining control over key sections of Lęborskie Przedmieście

---

31   J. Voelker, *Ostatnie dni…*, p. 87.
32   A. Sroga, *Na drodze…*, p. 194.
33   L. Saint-Loup Louis, *Les hérétiques…*, p. 306.
34   It is possible that his name was Francke.
35   R. Forbes, *For Europe…*, p. 360.

resulted in a group of SU-76 self-propelled guns from the Polish 3rd Armoured Artillery Squadron being sent to the area. Their 76.2mm cannons punched holes in the cemetery wall, but one of the SU-76s was lost during the operation, destroyed by either a *Panzerfaust* or a *Geballte-Ladung* grenade.

After several hours of bitter fighting, with neither side managing to gain a significant advantage,[36] the soldiers of the 7th Polish Infantry Regiment again asked for support. This time, a 122mm M38 howitzer from the 2nd Division of the 8th Artillery Regiment was sent to the church, towed by an American Studebaker US6 truck in Polish service. It was brought there by an NCO, Zenon Stein, who reported subsequent events to the author in October 2010:

> Our battery was deployed on the road to Białogard Church [St George's Church]. It was almost taken, but next to it was a small street to the left, currently No. 8 Primary School, and there the Germans defended themselves. On the other side, where there are now gardens, there was a cemetery, also full of German soldiers. Just then the battery commander called me, gave me a cannon and told me to go there and then report to an officer who would show me the target. I took the gun, got in the Studebaker car, passed the barricade in the culvert area on the road to Białogard and drove roughly to the the church. There, I didn't really know what to do. I checked in. The ensign showed me a target – a house in which the Germans sat, about 150–200 metres from me. The gun was erected across the road, facing the target. They started to shoot at us from the cemetery. The soldiers fired two or three shots and hit the house. It was obvious [from] how the Germans were escaping from it.

Stein also mentioned that many of the Poles, including himself, were surprised that enemy soldiers leaving the cemetery used a language other than German.[37] It should be presumed that they were the French from the assault groups.

The cemetery and the church of St George were finally seized by Polish troops on 11 March. Over the next 24 hours, the area was combed by soldiers of the 7th and 18th Polish Infantry Regiments. At the same time, elements of the French Compagnie de Marche moved from tenement houses in Koszalińska Street to the nearby gasworks. There, in order to raise the morale of the men, *SS-Obersturmführer* Ludwig organized a ceremony to posthumously award Iron Cross 1st and 2nd Class medals to honour those who lost their lives in the previous hours.

Some of his men, however, had already been captured, and were being held in the church they had recently defended. Alojzy Sroga remembers these exhausted French Grenadiers: "They settled down on the altar steps, in confessionals and benches …

---

36   A. Sroga, *Na drodze…*, p. 194.
37   Zenon Stein memoirs, recorded in 2010 and preserved in author's archives.

They ate, drank, spit, threw the heaviest curses. Some mumbled over graves."[38] *Waffen-Sturmführer* Pierre Werner, who previously commanded the artillery platoon of the *58. Waffen-Grenadier Regiment der SS*, was taken prisoner and taken to the headquarters of the 3rd Polish Infantry Division of Romuald Traugutt. Probably wanting to mislead the enemy, while also not knowing the current state of the *Compagnie de Marche*, Werner informed his interrogators that three French battalions, each of four 60-strong companies, were fighting as part of the *Festung Kolberg* garrison.[39]

Polish Army soldiers talk with German prisoners of war in the last days of the battle for Kołobrzeg. Perhaps in the group immortalized in this photograph there were also Frenchmen from the *33. Waffen-Grenadier Division der SS Charlemagne*. (Museum of Polish Arms in Kołobrzeg Archives)

At 0630 hours on 12 March, after two hours of continuous artillery shelling of the city, cars with megaphones appeared around the gasworks. For the next 40 minutes, a German-language speech flowed toward the soldiers who were manning the facility, a fragment of which was: "Soldiers, end the hopeless fight. Your leader has betrayed you. Our forces are already near Berlin ... Your hour has come." In response, the Frenchmen opened fire on the Poles with every means they had. A French assault

38   A. Sroga, *Na drodze...*, pp. 173–74.
39   Ibid., p. 283.

group was also sent to the church of St George, but they were unable to set fire to the ruins of the building.[40]

The following day, under direct fire from at least one Polish 122mm howitzer, the Germans and French were forced out of the ruins of the gas plant. This day was the last on which Hempel's unit offered any combat value.[41] From that day onward, the burden of fighting in the Śródmieście region rested on the shoulders of improvised groups of soldiers, often barely a dozen strong. The fighting in Lęborskie Przedmieście was some of the bloodiest during the entire battle for Kołobrzeg. German losses, and consequently those of the Frenchmen, are difficult to calculate. The scale of casualties during the several-day struggle can be seen by looking at the losses suffered by the 18th Polish Infantry Regiment. This unit's numbers dropped significantly during their several hours of fighting on the front line: They reported 135 dead (including 11 officers), 283 wounded and 77 missing.[42]

Calls for surrender were put forward by the Soviet–Polish forces to the fortress headquarters at 1530 hours on 14 March, the tenth day of the siege, but were completely ignored by *Oberst* Fullriede. Consequently, the fighting, which was moving closer to the city centre by the hour, entered its next phase.

Only incomplete data about what occurred with French *Compagnie de Marche* – or rather its individual platoons and teams which faced the enemy without communications – over the following days was collated by Johannes Volker, author of the German version of subsequent fighting in the city. Referring to the memories of Kołobrzeg inhabitant Otto Hannemann, Volker writes that on the day when the surrender of *Festung Kolberg* was demanded, a group of Frenchmen took positions in the basement of a tenement house at today's Jan Paweł II Alley. They directed their weapons into the yard, creating an improvised strongpoint. Most probably, all of them died during an attack on the house by a Polish assault group.

Another unit of *33. Waffen-Grenadier Division der SS* conducted activities in the ruins of buildings located between Michała Drzymały, Edmunda Łopuskiego and Strzelecka Streets. Initially, they organized positions for small arms and *Panzerfausts* in windowless openings, but at the request of civilians protecting themselves in adjacent flats, and despite artillery fire and airstrikes, they moved to the so-called

40   J. Voelker, *Ostatnie dni...*, p. 101. A note about the assault group's departure to Polish positions also appeared in the monograph on the battle of Kołobrzeg by Alojzy Sroga. However, he assigned it to 11 March. The following description of the attack on the church of St George was given in this publication: "In the breach there are two Nazis' sashes. They are in helmets, weapons on their shoulders, but they carry canisters. It is not difficult to guess what is in them. There is a moment behind the bend .... Two shots are fired, two broken corpses remain. Gasoline tanks clatter on the pavement." A. Sroga, *Na drodze...*, p. 252.

41   Ł. Gładysiak, *Batalion Alarmowy...*, p. 5.

42   Compared to the 1,600 Polish soldiers of the 18th Infantry Regiment in February 1945, only some 300 remained capable of combat at the end of operations in Lęborski Przedmieście. A. Sroga, *Na drodze...*, p. 312.

'Knischewski House', which is located near today's complex of hotels and economics schools in Kołobrzeg. To stop the Polish infantry from entering the area, they also set fire to a street barrier built of carts and beams abandoned by fleeing civilians. Direct contact with the enemy took place here on the night of 14–15 March. The grenadiers retreated and set up an observation and firing point at the Doberick Photographic Plant. Eventually, their resistance was broken. To date, it has not been possible to determine how many of *SS-Obersturmführer* Ludwig's men escaped, were taken prisoner or fell in battle.[43] Thanks to one participant in these events, Willy Ganzel, what is known is that after the Poles captured the area, civilians were led under guard to an assembly point in Lęborski Przedmieście, and from there to a transit camp in Obroty 7km south of the city.[44]

The junction of Edmunda Łopuskiego Street and Jan Paweł II Alley in Kołobrzeg (Kolberg) in February 2017, where on 14 March 1945, French *Waffen-SS* soldiers installed a burning barricade. (Łukasz Gładysiak)

When discussing the 10th day of the battle for the city, it is worth recalling the accusation made by Alojzy Sroga in 1980 against the French soldiers. This concerned the macabre discovery made by soldiers of the Polish 14th Infantry Regiment in one

---

43   J. Voelker, *Ostatnie dni...*, pp. 113–15.
44   Tamże, p. 120.

of the basements of the so-called 'Red Barracks', a complex located at what is now Jedności Narodowej Street. Charred bodies were found there of soldiers of the Polish regiment's 7th Company, including its commander, deputy-officer Marek Kahane. Recalling the memories of compatriots participating in the fighting, Sroga noted: "In one of the cellars, thirteen wire-bound corpses were found, bearing clear signs of pouring gasoline and arson. They must have died in cruel torture. After the first shock, the soldiers begin to look more closely, but yes – the remains of Polish uniforms. The least burned face and clothing was of the commanding officer." It was claimed that they had been burned alive two days earlier, and that members of the French *Compagnie de Marche* had committed the crime.[45] This seems unlikely, since it was established that the majority of the accused were involved in the defence of positions located elsewhere, in the eastern part of Kołobrzeg.

On 15-16 March, there were continuous retreats and thinning of the ranks of the French grenadiers – first towards the train station, and then the spa and port district. Although the unit tried to raise the morale of the staff of *Heeresgruppe Weichsel*, which in the battle log and official communications expressed appreciation for the Frenchmen's heroic actions,[46] their fate, as well as that of the entire *Festung Kolberg*, was sealed. Less than 48 hours before the surrender, *Waffen-Sturmführer* Blank led the last counterattack of the *Compagnie de Marche* towards today's Jagiellońska Street. Others broke through the Parsęta estuary from the south-west, but they were trapped in the ruins of buildings bordering the pre-war firing range of the German *4. Infanterie Regiment*.[47] On the 12th day of fighting, the order to prepare for a boldly planned evacuation by sea reached those at the casino, which included a disarmed group of Frenchmen, who had so far been involved in rear area operations. Many of them were exhausted, suffered from dysentery and could barely move. The lack of drinking water affected the health of all members of the fortress garrison and thousands of civilians. Some were so thirsty that they drew water from the corpse-strewn Parsęta, which only worsened the spread of poisoning.

By 17 March, no more than 60 troops from the *Compagnie de Marche* were still able to conduct any military activities. Most of them were on the eastern flank and the last line of defence in Kołobrzeg, most probably in the area of today's Regional Culture Centre of Zbigniew Herbert at Solna Street and Teatralny Park. As Jean Mabire suggests, during this period the command of the unit was in the hands of *SS-Untersturmführer* Büller. *SS-Obersturmführer* Ludwig underwent a nervous breakdown and fled to the *Festung Kolberg* staff, from where he was sent to the *4. Infanterie Regiment* casino. It seems he was given the task of commanding the remnants of the *Charlemagne* Division and leading them towards the port.[48]

---

45   A. Sroga, *Na drodze...*, pp. 425–26.
46   R. Forbes, *For Europe...*, p. 362.
47   R. Landwehr, *French Volunteers...*, p. 76.
48   J. Mabire, *La Division...*, p. 489.

Fort Münde in Kołobrzeg (Kolberg) – nowadays with a lighthouse on it, built shortly after the battle ended. This was the place where, on the night of 17–18 March 1945, the French *Waffen-SS* fight for the city finally ended. (Museum of the Polish Arms in Kołobrzeg Archives)

That same day, at 0900 hours, contrary to the orders of Adolf Hitler, Fullriede decided to evacuate his surviving units by sea. From now on, resistance would last only as long as the cover of the escaping civilians required, but no longer than the following morning. At 1500 hours, the fortress staff sent a report to the command of the German *3. Panzerarmee*, informing them about the tragic situation of the garrison and the commandant's decision. In response, a message was received about the temporary inability of *General der Panzertruppe* Hasso von Manteuffel, who commanded the army from 10 March 1945, to respond to the report.[49] This is nowadays interpreted as tacit consent for them to leave their posts.

The last act of fighting for *Festung Kolberg* took place in a tragic atmosphere. Both retreating German troops and columns of civilians heading to the Baltic shore were the target of artillery shelling. *Waffen-Sturmmann* Marotin recalled:

> We all rushed towards the mouth of the Parsęta, where hastily constructed bridges led escaping from the fortress to the decks of ships mooring in the sea. The whole was guarded by the crew of Fort Münde, built of red brick [Fort Ujście today, with a lighthouse], which was supposed to be the last point of

49   J. Voelker, *Ostatnie dni…*, p. 133.

resistance in this part of the city. Ivan [Marotin, like most soldiers of the *Charlemagne* Division, did not distinguish between Soviet and Polish units fighting in Pomerania] wedged into one of the main streets leading to the port, which also had railroad tracks [today' Towarowa Street]. He hit the last German barricades twice. Old men from [the] *Volkssturm* also fought with us; the unit with which I had been fighting for several days had reduced to twenty capable soldiers ... On the night of March 17–18, we stood on the beach at the foot of the said fort. The barricades [were composed] mainly [of everyday items such as furniture]. We saw boats approaching in our direction. Fearful of [grounding], they stopped several dozen metres from the shore. To get to them we had to run on very unstable wooden gangways. We were all extremely tired. The man running before me suddenly sank into the water in complete silence.[50]

On the penultimate day of fighting, at around 1700 hours, Polish soldiers finally broke through in the area of Fort Waldenfels, located at the end of today's Fredry Street and the race track, launching a decisive attack to the west. The beach and the entrance to the port were fired on by Soviet *Katyusha* rocket launchers. In the area of today's lighthouse, where the largest number of Germans gathered – both soldiers and civil refugees – panic broke out. They anxiously observed that more ships and boats were sailing out to sea. Every rumour about the arrival of another vessel caused the crowd to surge from improvised shelters, usually located in the basements of port buildings, to the waterfront. During these movements, many people, especially the elderly and children, were trampled, crushed or pushed into the icy waters of the Parsęta. Horses ran in panic around the streets, causing additional injuries.[51]

In the confusion, evacuation attempts continued. Alojzy Sroga suggests that the first group of Frenchmen left Kolobrzeg that day. They were boarded together with representatives of the Reich Railways and the Todt Organization.[52] Between 13 and 20 soldiers of the *Compagnie de Marche* were among the last uniformed men who got off the shore after the wooden gangways wobbled into the waves. The scene was described by author Johannes Volker:

> From the dock, Kołobrzeg looked like one big sea of flames. On the night of March 18, the city burned [along] its full width. At Lindenalle [modern Spacerowa Street], wagons with ammunition on the [railway] tracks exploded with a deafening bang. In Teifke's warehouse barracks on the same street, hundreds of gas barrels flew into the air for eight hours .... The sea was calm. Above all, the cloud vault was swirling high – blood red above the city and dark

50   R. Forbes, *For Europe...*, p. 364.
51   J. Voelker, *Ostatnie dni...*, p. 53.
52   A. Sroga, *Na drodze...*, p. 593.

black and blue in the north. Above Kołobrzeg, a black cloud of smoke rose, which soldiers and refugees could see from ships for a long time."[53]

During the late afternoon of 18 March, Corporal Franciszek Niewidziajło, a soldier of the 1st Polish Army, threw into the Baltic a wedding ring symbolizing the 'marriage' of the 1st and 2nd Polish Armies. This old maritime tradition was a symbol for the retaking by the Poles of the Pomeranian coast. Survivors of the *33. Waffen-Grenadier Division der SS Charlemagne* who managed to escape from the mouth of the Parsęta sailed westwards. They were afraid of becoming the target of Soviet submarines or aviation prowling the coastal area. However, they disembarked safely in Świnoujście. From the group of some 600 Frenchmen who found themselves in Kołobrzeg when the siege began, only 30 remained ready for action after two weeks of fighting.[54]

Kołobrzeg harbour entrance just after it was seized by Polish Army forces. This was the last part of the German defensive linse during the battle for the city. *Charlemagne* Division troops broke through to the harbour on the eve of *Festung Kolberg*'s collapse. (Museum of Polish Arms in Kołobrzeg Archives)

53   J. Voelker, *Ostatnie dni...*, p. 140.
54   R. Landwehr, *French Volunteers...*, pp. 76–77.

Following the end of the Second World War, the attitude of the French grenadiers was summarized by *SS-Obergruppenführer* Felix Steiner: "The French gave Kolberg so many proofs of courage that, if only the deeds from this period of fighting were mentioned, they deserve full immortality in the annals of military history ... Also there, volunteers wrote an interesting but lesser-known chapter of the history of French arms."[55] Fritz Fullriede also expressed admiration for the French troops.[56]

Not all men of *Charlemagne* Division managed to be evacuated by ship in the last days of the battle for *Festung Kolberg*. To date, at least two examples of attempts to escape from the besieged city by land are known. The first was undertaken by 18-year-old *Waffen-Grenadier* François de Lannurien, son of General Barazer de Lannurien, one of the main proponents of the commitment of the conquered French Third Republic to a pan-European crusade against Soviet Russia. Wandering about the ruins of the city, de Lannurien was captured by Polish forces, then found himself at an as yet undetermined collection point for prisoners in a forest near Kołobrzeg. Together with a group of German troops led by an officer in the *Kriegsmarine*, he managed to hide and wait for the POW column to be marched away. Over the next 15 days, the group moved west on foot for more than 100km, reaching Stepnica (Stepenitz). They managed to evade enemy units on several occasions, although de Lannurien was hampered by injuries to his back and foot. Despite temperatures hovvering around freezing, they managed to swim across the Oder. They finally met up with a *Wehrmacht* detachment in the Police (Politz) area. Most of the men, suffering from frostbite, were taken to a field hospital to recover.[57]

Less fortunate were a half-dozen Frenchmen, led by two unknown *Waffen-Unterscharführer* into the region of Stary Borek (Altbork), 6km southwest of Kołobrzeg. We know what happened next thanks to the writings of one of the *Charlemagne* Division members, Michel Cisey, translated by Jan Rutkiewicz for Polish Ośrodek Karta in Warsaw in 2006. It is worth quoting in detail:

> There were six of us left, we hid in a barn. At dawn, a mounted patrol stopped in the yard. The riders jumped off the horses, talked to the frightened 'bauer' and headed straight for our hideout. We heard the lock of [their weapons] and the German shout: 'Hands up! Get out!' We had no choice. We slipped off the heap and were immediately positioned by soldiers against the wall of the barn and wept. They were not Germans ... They were not interested in our weapons, but they told us to empty our pockets immediately. In this way I got rid of the watch, fountain pen, razor, wallet and other small things that I managed to keep so far ... It was obvious that execution was inevitable. I felt no fear, however. It's a matter of nervousness, not courage. Lack of fear allowed me to observe soldiers

55   F. Steiner., *Ochotnicy Waffen-SS...*, p. 230–31.
56   J. Voelker, *Ostatnie dni...*, p. 146.
57   R. Forbes, *For Europe...*, p. 366.

I have never seen up close ... Then I saw the Russians – not a Soviet [horde], but Russian people. I was curious about them. They should have killed us, but they didn't kill us. On the contrary, they enjoyed our watches and lighters. They seemed to be kids playing with objects that no child would be interested in in France ... We were rushed towards the command post. Along the way, we realized that we were dealing not with Russians, but with Poles, which did not impress us much.

Then prisoners were then interrogated, being spared no insults or beatings, but their lives were spared, which, if you believe Cisey's words, was helped by a recitation of a Catholic prayer in Latin. The next stage of captivity, at Karlino, was well known to soldiers of the *33. Waffen-Grenadier Division der SS Charlemagne*:

Accompanied by two escorts, we set off towards Karlino. It was a gruesome walk, full of tragic memories. Only a month ago I travelled this route, but in completely different circumstances ... The road was [covered] with a monstrous bundle of scorched iron, decomposing corpses, scattered weapons, and all this was covered in drying mud. On both sides, up to the horizon, was a battlefield littered with tanks, which were now still and gutted. The earth was strewn with greenish, distorted and pitifully twisted corpses. Their faces had no expression of deadly peace, for they belonged to those whose lives had long been an idyll.

During the march, the French met a group of Polish soldiers accompanying delegates from Warsaw, Julia Skarbińska and Jan Roszczyński, to the Kołobrzeg area. They were accompanied by Sergeant Józef Rybicki, a self-proclaimed photo-chronicler of the Polish 4th Infantry Division of Jan Kiliński, thanks to which we can follow these events today in photographs preserved in the archives of the Ośrodek Karta in Warsaw and the Museum of Polish Arms in Kołobrzeg. Michel Cisay later observed:

A civilian with an automatic weapon in his hand came from behind us. Meanwhile, a sergeant [Józef Rybicki], probably for practice, shot down a few porcelain insulators stuck on telegraph poles, and the escorts were already cleaning the roadside ditch of branches and broken crates. The trench was about the width of a lying man ... Then the escorts aimed at us, aiming at our heads. The sergeant took a few steps back as usual, to give the command '*Pal!*' ['Fire!' in Polish]. The civilian was also ready ... The woman [Julia Skarbińska] was walking away slowly. Suddenly the sergeant made a gesture – 'wait a minute!' Something black flashed in his hand – the shutter snapped. 'It's for propaganda,' he said, as an excuse. ... The escorts threw their weapons on their shoulders, as did the civilian. The woman turned back to us. Everyone got in the car and drove.

A series of photographs taken in March 1945, in the vicinity of Stary Borek (Altbork) village near Kołobrzeg (Kolberg), depicting the meeting of a group of prisoners from the *33. Waffen-Grenadier Division der SS Charlemagne* with soldiers of the Polish Army and a delegation of Poles from Warsaw. The scene immortalized in the pictures was described many years after the end of the war by Michel Cisay. These are the only known photographs showing members of the French unit during the fighting in the area. Note the details of the uniforms, including the unusual footwear of one of the non-commissioned officers. (Museum of Polish Arms in Kołobrzeg Archives)

On reaching Karlino, the French prisoners were passed over to Soviet soldiers. Following a brutal interrogation by agents of the infamous *Smersh* counter-intelligence unit, they were sent, along with other German POWs, to clean up the city and bury victims of earlier fighting:

> Our work was to bury everything that once lived – corpses of men, women, children, cattle. What might seem repugnant was a blessing to us prisoners. When we were ordered to dig pits in the centre of the town, it turned out that we found cellars filled with food and drink. It is hard to imagine the quantities of victuals that the [protective] German hosts stored. Our Polish escorts did not refuse to supply us with what we wanted."

Then, probably by this time in April, Cisay and his companions were sent to a POW camp deep inside the Soviet Union, most likely Tambov nad Cna, where, shortly after the fall of the Third Reich, most of the captured men of *SS-Brigadeführer* Gustav Krukenberg were also sent. Cisay was released in 1946 after a relatively short time in captivity.[58]

As the author managed to determine, after the battle for Kołobrzeg was over, the captured French were temporarily detained in ad hoc places of internment at the intersection of Kościelna and 4th Infantry Division Streets (next to today's church of St Andrzej Bobola) in Gościno and in farm buildings next to the palace in Stanomino, where it seems that at least two of them died and were buried. In April, prisoners held in the second location were temporarily transferred to Choszczno and then to Poznań. After the unconditional surrender of the Third Reich, they were transported to Warsaw, and from there to POW camps in the USSR.

Apart from the group of Frenchmen who were included in the *Festung Kolberg* garrison, after the final breakup of the *33. Waffen-Grenadier Division der SS Charlemagne* at the confluence of the Parsęta and Radwia Rivers, the fight was continued by men of the head of the 1st Battalion of the *Régiment de Marche*, *Waffen-Hauptsturmführer* Henri Fenet. After joining the group, accompanied by weapons from the *Belgard an der Persante Régiment de Marche* that had broken down near Białogard, with elements of the *Korpsgruppe Munzel*, a decision was made to march from Międzyrzecz northwards, directly to the Baltic, to catch up with the core of *Korpsgruppe von Tettau* heading towards Rewal.

The march took place on 7 March, passing the border between today's Kołobrzeg and Gryfice districts, along National Road 6 to the village of Pniewo (Pinnow) and. another 12km east of Gryfice to Natolewice (Nebelfitz). There, they established contact with the formation led by *General der Infanterie* von Tettau. Instead of the originally planned counterattack towards Gryfice, which became bogged down after

58   M. Cisay, *Francuski esesman*, [w:] Kwartalnik Historyczny Ośrodka Karta, Nr 48 (Warsaw: 2006), pp. 81-86.

The stables in Stanomino (Standemin) in November 2016 – one of the places where in March 1945 the French *Waffen-SS* POWs captured by Soviet and Polish forces were sent. (Łukasz Gładysiak)

only 3km, the exhausted Frenchmen were loaded onto trucks. After dark, they checked in to Przybiernów (Pribbernow). By this time the *Korpsgruppe* was almost completely devoid of radio communication, so its troops were not able to send reports to or receive orders from the staff of the German *3. Panzerarmee*, to which it was formally included.

At dawn the next day, Fenet was ordered to move to Kamień Pomorski. This task was verified after contact with local civilians, who reported that the city was already besieged by the Red Army. The unit turned back to the Baltic Sea and then set off south of Trzebiatów. At one of the crossings on the Redze River, the advance guard spotted the crews of two Soviet T-34/85 tanks encamped, not expecting any attack. As ordered by von Tettau, no action was taken against them, so that the march to the sea would continue to escape enemy attention. Soon after, one of the column's vehicles exploded after driving over a mine, as a result of which seven Frenchmen lost their lives. The column halted in the late afternoon of 8 March at Czaplin Wielki (Gross Zaplin). Along the way, they avoided fighting again, despite a battle between German and Soviet forces being fought practically along their route in the village of Górzyca (Görke). At around 1830 hours, the group set out again via Chomętowo (Gumtow) towards Czaplin Mały (Klein Zaplin). The following morning, having travelled some 11km, they arrived at Niechorze (Ostseebad Horst) on the Baltic coast.[59]

59   R. Forbes, *For Europe...*, pp 366–67.

One of the most dramatic and unbelievable events during the Pomeranian campaign commenced on 9 March. On a narrow patch of land that was bordered to the north by the sea, between 20,000 and 40,000 people – soldiers and civilians – gathered around *Korpsgruppe von Tettau*. From the south, elements of the Soviet 15th and 16th Cavalry Divisions rushed towards the bridgehead, followed by the 79th Rifle Corps, while the Polish 2nd Infantry Division and the 13th Armoured Artillery Regiment closed in from the west. Around 1100 hours, the staff of *Korpsgruppe von Tettau* reported to *Heeresgruppe Weichsel* that they were surrounded. The boundary of its defence was marked out on the line from Pustkowo (Pustschow), where the brickworks became the key point, through Karnice (Karnitz) and Włodarka (Voigtshagen) to the foot of Königsberg hill, which is located in a coastal forest about halfway between Niechorze and Mrzeżyno.

Soldiers believed to be from the *Charlemagne* Division marching somewhere in Pomerania in early 1945. (Private archive)

During the early afternoon, when most German sub-units and elements of the former 1st Battalion of the *Régiment de Marche* were preparing for the expected evacuation, a *Fi-156 Storch* reconnaissance aircraft landed near the Niechorze lighthouse. On board were two representatives of the staff of the *3. Panzerarmee*: *Major* Kron and *Feldwebel* Borgelt.[60] They told von Tettau that escape by sea was impossible due to

---

60   M. Klasik, *Ziemia Kamieńska przed 65 laty* <http://www.uzdrowisko.kamienpomorski.pl/news.php?readmore=1076> (Accessed 31 August 2012).

the involvement of most vessels in evacuation activities in the Kolobrzeg area.[61] The original plan to counterattack from Wolin towards Dziwnów (*Dievenow*) to break the encirclement was abandoned. The only option seemed to be an attempt to cross a narrow coastal belt. After the meeting, *Major* Kron sent a report to *General der Panzertruppe* von Manteuffel which described the critical situation of von Tettau's men:

> Tettau sits in Niechorze and has a bridgehead 20km wide and 10km long … On the section from Niechorze to Chomętów inclusive there are elements of the *'Holstein' Panzer Division* without tracked vehicles, from there to Włodarka *Infanterie Division 'Pommern'*, [and] the Latvian *15. Grenadier Division der SS* further to Mrzeżyno. There are about fifty thousand people on the bridgehead, half of which are civilians and half of them soldiers. The 1st and 2nd Battalions of the *5. Jäger Division* passed through Golczewo and are now standing near Szczecin. Heavy equipment: thirty artillery barrels, slightly less 8.8cm guns, [plus] self-propelled guns. There is no exact data for this. No anti-tank guns and tanks. *'Holstein' Panzer Division* completely annihilated … Only one five-ton bridge near Dziwnów! You must use ferries!

On 10 March, when the enemy launched an attack towards the Baltic shore around Trzebiatów, the first group of German soldiers and some of the men of *Waffen-Hauptsturmführer* Fenet (it is difficult to define clearly which) moved along the dunes towards Rewal. The 5km journey was made without incident, due to the tying up of enemy forces by elements of the regiment formed from the pupils of the *Wehrmacht* 4th Artillery School, and they arrived at Rewal at 1700 hours.

The breakout of the remainder of *Korpsgruppe von Tettau* along the same route began the next afternoon. At around 1550 hours on 11 March, *Oberst* Eismann from the group's staff managed to establish telephone contact with the *OKH*. Guidelines regarding the group's escape were confirmed, with the troops protected by fire from *Kriegsmarine* ships, including the heavy cruiser *Admiral Scheer* and the destroyers *Z-31, Z-38* and *Paul Jacobi*.[62]

Meantime, Soviet and Polish forces began to attack von Tettau's positions. *Feldwebel* Borgelt recalled:

> I was standing on the cliff with the general. We saw the advancing Russians, [and] a deafening scream pierced the air: '*Urra!*' Then von Tettau turned to one of his officers: 'It's time, gentlemen, let's show them something they will remember for the rest of their lives.' We began to move towards the attackers, conducting fire in silence, almost like in a shooting range. I took the rifle from

61   H. Lindenblatt, *Pommern 1945…*, p. 263.
62   *Idem., Dziwnowski Front…*

one of the wounded. For the first time during the war, I was so close to the enemy. The Russians opened fire with mortars, but grenades flew over the column, exploding on the beach. I turned around and felt my stomach squeeze. Behind the army, a large crowd of civilians followed, shells exploding among them ... I have never seen so many bodies – civilians, German and Soviet soldiers. I remember especially the last ones, as if piled on top of each other. Between the corpses I saw dead horses, overturned carts, on which refugees travelled, weapons and equipment ... The sight of completely exhausted soldiers who had not eaten anything for several days could cause depression. However, there was nothing as terrible as women's expressions, some threw small children into the waves, having no strength to carry them away.[63]

French grenadiers were amongst the group that began its slow procession, harassed by constant fire not only from small arms and self-propelled guns, but also shells of larger calibre fired by the Polish 5th Heavy Artillery Brigade deployed around Kamień Pomorski. Losses were increasing, with some caused by German ships. Injured French, who called for help from the crowd, tried to find members of the improvised medical column led by *Waffen-Unsterturmführer* Leune and Dr Métaise. Having lost the road, the unit turned towards the dunes and entered into a crossfire. Miraculously escaping death, the Frenchmen reached the road running along the coast, probably today's Provincial Road 102. There, the bodies of comrades were abandoned and they set off further west. Robert Forbes reports that soon after, the medical unit encountered a defeated Soviet column with two destroyed T-34/85 tanks. There was also a truck, in which *Waffen-Oberscharführer* Boucret found parcels with food rations from the United States, sent to the Eastern Front as part of Allied assistance to the Red Army. The food was quickly divided between the group. At around 1500 hours, the troops managed to establish contact with German units near Dziwnów, among whom was *SS-Brigadeführer* Krukenberg. An anecdote associated with this meeting with the commander of the still formally existing *33. Waffen-Grenadier Division der SS Charlemagne* had it that the reprimanded Dr Métais over his appearance, having lost his gloves and the pockets of his uniform being too full.[64]

Meantime, the exodus had reached the beach. From Rewal, *Korpsgruppe von Tettau*, the remains of the Fenet's battalion and a significant number of civilians marched through Pobierowo (Poberow) and Łukęcin (Lüchtenthin). The group had to maintain a narrow file to continue. An assault squad was selected from among the French, with *SS-Hauptsturmführer* Jauss at its head. Despite considerable fatigue, with a bold attack using rifle-fire, he first eliminated a camouflaged enemy heavy machine-gun position, and then, personally leading the assault with a hand grenade, destroyed another, this time in a house on the dunes. At 0400 hours on 12 March, the

63   Ch. Duffy, *Red Storm...*, pp. 197-98.
64   R. Forbes, *For Europe...*, p. 372.

Frenchmen first encountered German units from Dziwnów.[65] Four hours later, they finally reach the city.[66]

Vessels docked all day at the port in Dziwnów, including 13 military ferries and six submarine hunters, then sailed to Świnoujście. Those who failed to get on board were forced to march west towards Międzyzdroje (Misdroy). That same day, Niechorze and the surrounding area were overrun by Soviet and Polish forces. Author Helmut Lindenblatt calculated that approximately 27,000 people, including 10,700 soldiers, withdrew from the Niechorze encirclement. They managed to save 28 artillery pieces of various calibres from destruction, including three anti-tank guns, and 180 machine guns.[67] *Korpsgruppe von Tettau*'s trek from Niechorze to Dziwnów was one of the most unbelievable episodes in the whole wartime history of *Provinz Pommern*.

The Pomeranian campaign ended for Fenet's men with the division broken down into small battlegroups, which set off separately along the northern shore of Wolin Island. Some of them passed through Międzywodzie (Heidebrink) and Świętouście (Swantuss) in the Kołczew (Kolzow) area. From there, along today's Voivodship Road 102, they headed for Międzyzdroje. The grenadiers were accompanied throughout by *SS-Brigadeführer* Krukenberg and *SS-Standartenführer* Zimmermann. The latter, who had an injured foot, used a bicycle found along the trail.[68] On the afternoon of 13 March, the reunited French unit, after covering over 70km on foot from Niechorze to the mouth of the Świna River, entered Świnoujście. Jean Mabire claims that, despite extreme exhaustion and significant shortcomings in uniforms, equipment and armament, the French entered the city in an orderly marching column, with a song on their lips, causing astonishment among their German comrades in arms.[69]

---

65   *Die Wehrmachtsberichte 1939–1945. Band 3...*, p. 483.
66   R. Forbes, *For Europe...*, p. 370.
67   H. Lindenblatt, *Pommern 1945...*, p. 274.
68   R. Forbes, *For Europe...*, p. 373.
69   J. Mabire, *Mourir á Berlin...*, p. 37.

Epilogue

After the Pomeranian campaign, the remnants of the *33. Waffen-Grenadier Division der SS Charlemagne* concentrated around Anklam in the German region of Mecklenburg, which is now about 45km west of the Polish border. All of *SS-Brigadeführer* Gustav Krukenberg's men who were capable of fighting congregatedin Jargelin, where the first grenadiers began to arrive on 8 March. Eight days later, *Waffen-Haupsturmführer* Henri Fenet, who was already one of the true divisional legends, joined his comrades-. At that time, of the original complement of about 4,500 men who began operations in Pomerania around Czarne at the end of February, slightly more than 700 – including 23 officers – remained capable of action. Many of them, including *SS-Standartenführer* Walter Zimmermann, were seriously wounded and receiving treatment in hospital.

On 18 March, the divisional commander left his soldiers for a day, heading to *Heeresgruppe Weichsel* headquarters at Prenzlau in Brandenburg. After delivering his report of the Pomeranian campaign, he returned to Jargelin, authorized by *Reichsführer-SS* Heinrich Himmler to grant promotions and decorations. The relevant ceremonies were organized on 19 March. Among those honoured were *Waffen-Hauptsturmführer* Fenet, who was approved for promotion from *Obersturmführer*, and *Standartenoberjunker* Labourdette, who was awarded first officer rank and the Iron Cross 1st Class. The same 2nd Class decoration was given to 16 other grenadiers, including *Waffen-Untersturmführer* Christian Martret, who had been responsible for the communications unit during the battles at Olszanów. –Further honours took place throughout the next week.

The remaining French grenadiers gathered at Anklam train station on 21 March, from where, once again without means of transport, they set off for Schwerinsburg, and from there to Sarnow, Friedland and Schöneck. Some 48 hours later, the troops found themselves at Stolpe, and the next day they arrived in Carpin.

Due to the increasingly dire situation for German troops on all fronts and the spectre of the Allies launching a direct attack towards Berlin, the *SS* Central Office issued a directive on 25 March reforming the French division into the *SS-Grenadier Regiment Charlemagne*, comprising two infantry battalions and a heavy battalion with an assault, anti-aircraft and anti-tank gun company. The whole was to be supplemented by a communications platoon, a platoon of sappers, a workshop platoon, and a supply column. The battle readiness of Krukenberg's regiment was to be achieved no later than 15 April.

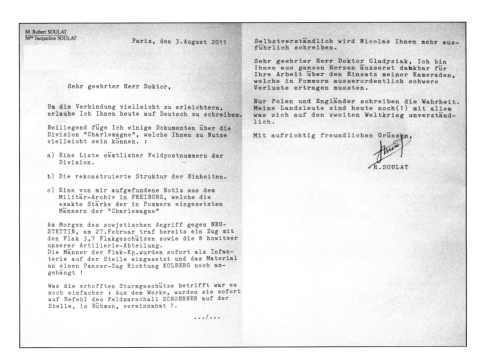

A letter from *Waffen-Rottenführer* Robert Soulat, attached staff company of the *Charlemagne* Division, sent to the author in early August 2011. Regular correspondence for the next two years resulted in obtaining a number of pieces of previously unknown information about the French group and its participation in battles in Pomerania in 1945. (Author's archives)

Stationed at the city of Neustrelitz, they were joined by a group of inexperienced soldiers who fled from France the previous year in fear of revenge from their countrymen. With their addition, by the end of March, the French unit numbered some 1,000 men. In the first days of April, 700 of them, as the *Sturm-Regiment der SS Charlemagne* , decided to voluntarily continue fighting for the Germans. Less than 400 of these reached Berlin for the final fight against the Red Army.

The sterling effort for Germany, not only for French but also for other foreign volunteers, against Soviet and Polish forces in the northern sector of the Eastern Front in early 1945 were not enough to prevent the destruction of the *Wehrmacht* in Pomerania. The exact losses suffered by the French *Waffen-SS* unit during the battles fought by *Heeresgruppe Weichsel* between January and the end of March 1945 seem impossible to determine today. During the turmoil associated with permanent retreat, it was often the case that no records were made. Field studies indicate that the fallen were not recorded using a basic piece of personal equipment, the *Erkennungsmarke* identity disc (the so-called dog tag), which would have allow their final fate to be determined. It can be assumed that to this day many French troops remain buried anonymously in mass or individual graves. The most persistent of them, but also the most fortunate, fought for Hitler's Third Reich until the last days of its existence. For some of them, this moment marked the beginning of another epic, no less dangerous than their efforts along the Baltic coast. It was marked by trying to find their way through enemy-occupied Germany and looking for a way home, where they often met with nothing but contempt from their compatriots, and in extreme cases even revenge. Many were rightly accused of treason and active collaboration. Many were sentenced to lengthy spells in prison or Soviet labour camps, including the infamous Tambov camp near the Tsna River, over 450km southeast of Moscow.

By virtue of the Yalta provisions, the majority of the former *Provinz Pommern* was situated within the borders of Poland. It is hoped that, regardless of the emotional attitude of the Polish people to the events of 1945 and their participants, activities there will continue to thoroughly investigate the era of German Pomerania and the formations involved in the region's capture and defence.

Appendix I

Select Biographies

Victor de Ghaisnes de Bourmont
(1907–45)

Victor de Ghaisenes de Borumont was born on 5 May 1907 on the Pontiva estate in the Breton department of Morbihan. His family, part of the French aristocracy, participated in the most significant events in the military history of their homeland: among Victor's ancestors were a marshal and parish priest, as well as the minister of war, Louis Auguste de Bourmont. Victor's father served as an officer in the 160th Infantry Regiment, and his uncle died during the Battle of Verdun in 1916. At the age of 20, Victor entered the Saint-Cyr Military Academy, from which he graduated in 1929 as a lieutenant. Upon the outbreak of the Second World War, he served in Tunisia as a captain of the French Foreign Legion.

In June 1940, he found himself in German captivity. After a short time, he declared his willingness to serve in the ranks of the German Army or units allied with it against the forces of General de Gaulle's Free French. He eventually joined the French Guard, commanding a unit in Lyon. At the beginning of 1944, he participated in the planning and implementation of actions directed against the resistance movement in the Glières region in Haute-Savoie, during which he commanded a separate unit codenamed 'E'.

In summer 1944, fearing arrested by the Allies or the revenge of his countrymen, he fled to Germany. In December, in the rank of *Waffen-Hauptsturmführer*, he was appointed commander of the *57. Waffen-Grenadier Regiment der SS*, being sent to fight defending Pomerania. After the reorganization of the *33. Waffen-Grenadier Division der SS 'Charlemagne'* in Białogard, he found himself in the staff of the Reserve Regiment. With them he took part in the break-out from Karlino, during which, probably on 5 March 1945, he was killed in action. A year later, French justice authorities in the Rhône department sentenced him *in absentia* to the death penalty for active collaboration.

Gustav Krukenberg
(1888–1980)

Gustav Krukenberg was born on 8 March 1888 in Bonn, in the family of a professor at the city's university and the daughter of a well-known German archaeologist, Alexander Coze. In 1907, he enlisted in the ranks of the German Army officer corps. Earlier, he earned his doctoral dissertation in law. During the First World War, serving as a staff officer at Sedan, he was promoted to the rank of captain. After the conflict, he worked at the Ministry of Foreign Affairs of the Weimar Republic, including as secretary of the head of the ministry. He also held managerial positions in German industry. From the mid-1920s, he ran the Paris office of the German–French Studies Commission. In 1932, he joined the National Socialist German Workers' Party (the Nazi Party), becoming a stormtrooper, moving to the *Allgemeine-SS* the following year. As a commissioner of radio stations, he became involved in propaganda.

Following the outbreak of the Second World War, he returned to service as a major, receiving an assignment to the staff of the occupation forces in the Netherlands, then in 1941 to the German military headquarters in occupied Paris. In December 1943, after serving for several months in the command of the Reich Economic Inspection Centre in Belarus, he was given the rank of *SS-Obersturmbannführer* and transferred to the ranks of the *Waffen-SS*. In January of the following year, he was among the staff of the *V Gebirgskorps* (5th Mountain Corps), where he was quickly promoted to *SS-Oberführer*. In May 1944, he became the chief of staff of the finally unformed *VI SS-Freiwilligen Korps*, and two months later the *SS* commander at the *Ostland Reichskommissariat*. Due to his fluent command of the French language and knowledge of the country's culture, Krukenberg was promoted to *SS-Brigadeführer* and appointed inspector of French units, and then the commander – under operational commander *Waffen-Oberführer* Edgar Puaud – of the *33. Waffen-Grenadier Division der SS 'Charlemagne'*. He held this position until the end of the unit's existence. On 25 April 1945, he additionally took command of the 'C' defence sector in Berlin. During the battles for the city, he also headed the *11. Freiwilligen-Grenadier Division der SS 'Nordland'*.

Twenty-four hours before the fall of Berlin, he managed to break out to the Dahlem district, where he went into hiding for a a week until found by Soviet soldiers. He remained in captivity in the USSR until 1956. He then returned to Germany and became involved in the Union of Returning from Captivity and Missing Persons. He also kept in touch with the French *'Charlemagne'* veterans until he died on 23 October 1980 in the Rhineland town of Bad Godesberg.

Historian Werner Coze, a cousin of Gustav Krukenberg, was a professor at the Reichs-University in Poznań, Poland (Posen during the German occupation). He was one of the leading propagators of the idea of National Socialism and the predestination of Germany to rule the world.

Edgar Puaud
(1889–1945)

Edgar Puaud was born on 29 October 1889 in the French city of Orleans. He graduated from Saint Maixent military academy as an NCO. He served as a lieutenant and then a captain at the front in the First World War. His bravery in battle earned him the *Croix de Guerre* and the *Légion d'honneur* – the highest French military award. In the 1920s, he joined the elite Saint-Cyr Military Academy, ultimately taking command of a battalion of the Foreign Legion as a major. At that time, he did not hide his royalist beliefs, which did not win him friends among the republican patriots.

Following the conquest of France by the Third Reich in 1940, he took the side of the puppet authorities in Vichy and remained in the armed forces. Two years later, he joined the ranks of the 638th Infantry Regiment formed under the auspices of the *Wehrmacht*, known as the Legion of French Volunteers against Bolshevism (LVF), which he commanded from 1943. On 10 August the following year, after being promoted to *Waffen-Oberführer*, he commanded – along with *SS-Brigadeführer* Gustav Krukenberg – the *Waffen-Grenadier Brigade der SS 'Charlemagne'*, which was expanded in early 1945 to the *33. Waffen-Grenadier Division der SS 'Charlemagne'*. He served with this formation in the February battles in Pomerania. During the reorganization of the group in Białogard, he headed the Reserve Regiment.

His eventual fate is shrouded in mystery. According to most historians, Edgar Puaud died on 6 March 1945, during Soviet shelling, shortly after the start of an attack on a column retreating south from Karlin, being buried soon after in a mass grave, perhaps near the village of Łęczynko. Another theory is that Puaud was only wounded and managed to escape, reaching Gryfice, where he was captured and killed by the Russians. A further thesis suggests that he survived the war and lived to old age under an assumed name somewhere in France or West Germany. The least likely claim is that he was imprisoned for many years in the USSR and went on to serve in the higher structures of the KGB in East Germany.

Emile Raybaud
(1910–95)

Emile Raybaud was born on 19 May 1910 in Trans, Provence. He studied from 1930–32 at the Saint-Cyr Military Academy, and after graduating was promoted to *sous-lieutenant* in the armed forces of the Third Republic. The outbreak of the Second World War found him as a *capitaine* in the *20e Bataillon de Chasseurs Alpins*. During the 1940 campaign, he participated in battles with German forces, including the Somme.

Following the conquest of France by the Third Reich, he took the side of the Vichy government. He joined the *Milice Française*, quickly rising through its ranks. In April 1943, he assumed command of a training centre for the organization's personnel located in the mountain resort of Uriage-les-Bains. He was also one of the organizers of large-scale actions carried out in February and March 1944 against troops of the *Maquis de Glières*, French resistance units operating in the department of Haute-Savoie, which were commanded by former officers of French alpine riflemen. In June 1944, he replaced Jean de Vaugelas as commander of the Vichy militia in Limousine, a month later taking command of the northern section of *Les Guardes Françaises* – a militia operating in the unoccupied territory of France in support of the Third Reich, being involved in the extermination of Jews.

Due to the progress made by the Western Allies and the spectre of retaliation by his countrymen, Raybaud fled to Germany. He was sent to the Wildflecken camp in November 1944 and gained the rank of *Waffen-Haupsturmführer*. In mid-February 1945, he became commander of the *58. Waffen-Grenadier Regiment der SS*. After the reorganization of the '*Charlemagne*' Division in Białogard, with the rank of *Waffen-Sturmbannführer* he headed the French *Regiment de Marche*, then commanded Karlino during the fighting in the city. Injured while visiting one of the defence positions, he was evacuated to Kolobrzeg and had a leg amputated. In recognition of his merits, he was awarded the Iron Cross 1st Class and was promoted to *Waffen-Obersturmbannführer*, but he only learned of these honours after the capitulation of the Third Reich.

After fighting in Europe, he returned to France and was arrested and accused by the Haute-Vienne justice system of active collaboration, including battles against the resistance. He was sentenced to death in 1946. He spent the next five years in a prison in Limoges before being pardoned and eventually released. He died aged 85 on 7 September 1995.

Eugène Vaulot
(1923–45)

Eugène Vaulot was born in Paris on 1 June 1923. When German forces invaded France in 1940, he was working as a technician-electrician. When the German authorities announced the enlistment of Frenchmen into the ranks of the Legion of French Volunteers against Bolshevism (LVF), he abandoned his occupation and was sent to the Eastern Front as part of this unit. In 1943, while a *corporel*, he was forced to suspend his military service because of wounds. Not wanting to part with the German Army, a year later he volunteered to serve in the ranks of *Schiffstammabteilung 28* in Świnoujście, becoming a *Waffen-Unterscharführer* and being sent to the camp in Wildflecken.

In the ranks of the 1st Staff Company (also known as the Company of Honour) of the *33. Waffen-Grenadier Division der SS 'Charlemagne'*, he fought through the entire Pomeranian campaign. After being evacuated from Szczecinek, he went to a new assembly point in Białogard and then to Koszalin. During this time, he was awarded the Iron Cross 1st Class. After the breakup of the division, he managed to get through occupied Denmark to Neustrelitz in Mecklenburg. He then went to fight for Berlin as part of the *SS-Sturmbataillon 'Charlemagne'*. In the final period of the battle in the encircled city, he managed to destroy eight Soviet tanks in one day, including six near the Reich Chancellery. On 29 April, during a ceremony organized at the Stadtmitte metro station, he was awarded the Knight's Cross of the Iron Cross. He is reported to have said then: "I fought with one dream, to be honoured with this decoration. I can die now." Vaulot was killed by a sniper three days later whilst attempting to break out of Berlin.

Appendix II

Waffen-SS foreign unit ranks and their British equivalents

Waffen-SS	British Army
SS (Waffen)-Grenadier	Private
SS (Waffen)-Obergrenadier	Private First Class
SS (Waffen)-Sturmmann	N/A
SS (Waffen)-Rottenführer	Corporal
SS (Waffen)-Unterscharführer	Sergeant
SS (Waffen)-Scharführer	Platoon Sergeant Major
SS (Waffen)-Oberscharführer	Company Sergeant Major
SS (Waffen)-Hauptscharführer	Battalion Sergeant Major
SS (Waffen)-Sturmscharführer	Regimental Sergeant Major
SS (Waffen)-Untersturmführer	Second Lieutenant
SS (Waffen)-Obersturmführer	Lieutenant
SS (Waffen)-Hauptsturmführer	Captain
SS (Waffen)-Sturmbannführer	Major
SS (Waffen)-Oberstrumbannführer	Lieutenant Colonel
SS (Waffen)-Standartenführer	Colonel
SS (Waffen)-Oberführer	N/A
SS (Waffen)-Brigadeführer	Brigadier
SS-Gruppenführer	Major General
SS-Obergruppenführer	Lieutentat General

Appendix III

Tables

Table 1: Alphabetical list of major Pomeranian cities and larger towns along the battle route of the *33. Waffen-Grenadier Division der SS 'Charlemagne'* in February, March, and April 1945

Polish (current) name	German (1945) name	Poviat	Voivodship	Period
Czarne	Hammerstein	Człuchowski	Pomorskie	Feb 1945
Białogard	Belgard an der Persante	Białogardzki	Zachodniopomorskie	March 1945
Gryfice	Greifenberg	Gryficki	Zachodniopomorskie	Feb–March 1945
Kamień Pomorski	Kammin	Kamieński	Zachodniopomorskie	March 1945
Karlino	Körlin	Białogardzki	Zachodniopomorskie	March 1945
Kołobrzeg	Kolberg	Kołobrzeski	Zachodniopomorskie	March 1945
Miastko	Rummelsburg	Bytowski	Pomorskie	Feb 1945
Połczyn Zdrój	Bad Polzin	Szczecinecki	Zachodniopomorskie	Feb 1945
Rewal	Rewahl	Gryficki	Zachodniopomorskie	March 1945
Sławno	Schlawe	Sławieński	Zachodniopomorskie	March 1945
Szczecinek	Neustettin	Szczecinecki	Zachodniopomorskie	Feb 1945
Świnoujście	Swinemünde	Świnoujście	Zachodniopomorskie	March 1945
Trzebiatów	Treptow an der Rega	Gryficki	Zachodniopomorskie	March 1945
Wolin	Wollin	Kamieński	Zachodniopomorskie	March 1945

Table 2: Origins of the *33. Waffen-Grenadier Division der SS 'Charlemagne'* personnel

Previous unit	Amount
8. SS-Sturmbrigade	1,000
LVF	1,200
Vichy Militia units	2,500
Navy and Naval Militia units	640
Paramilitary organizations	2,500
Total:	7,840

Table 3: *33. Waffen-Grenadier Division der SS 'Charlemagne'* sub-units and commanders after the reorganization in Białogard (Belgard an der Persante), 1 March 1945

33. Waffen-Grenadier Division der SS 'Charlemagne'	
Divisional Headquarters: Commander: Operational commander:	 *SS-Brigadeführer* Gustav Krukenberg *Waffen-Oberführer* Edgar Puaud
SS-Marsch-Regiment 33	
Regimental Headquarters: Commander: Aide:	 *Waffen-Sturmbannführer* Emile Raybaud *Waffen-Obersturmführer* Marcel Baudouin
1 Bataillon: Commander: Aide: *1. Kompanie* Commander: *2. Kompanie* Commander: *3. Kompanie* Commander: *4. Kompanie* Commander:	 *Waffen-Hautpsturmführer* Henri Fenet *Waffen-Standartenoberjunker* Jean Labourdette *Waffen-Obersturmführer* Roumegous *Waffen-Oberscharführer* Lucien Hennecart Unknown *Waffen-Oberscharführer* Covreur
2. Bataillon Commander: Aide: *1. Kompanie* Commander: *2. Kompanie* Commander: *3. Kompanie* Commander: *4. Kompanie* Commander:	 *Waffen-Hauptsturmführer* Jean Bosompierre *Waffen-Obersturmführer* Georges Wagner *Waffen-Hauptscharführer* Eric Walter *Waffen-Untersturmführer* Yves Rigeade Unknown *Waffen-Obersturmführer* Jean Français

SS-Reserve-Regiment 33	
Regimental Headquarters:	
Commander:	*Waffen-Sturmbannführer* Victor de Bourmount
Aide:	*Waffen-Untersturmführer* Christian Martret
1. Bataillon:	
Commander:	*Waffen-Hauptsturmführer* Emile Monneuse
Aide:	*Waffen-Untersturmführer* Jean Brazier
1. Kompanie Commander:	*Waffen-Untersturmführer* Erdozain
2. Kompanie Commander:	Unknown
3. Kompanie Commander:	*Waffen-Untersturmführer* Pierre Hug
4. Kompanie Commander:	*Waffen-Hauptscharführer* Terret
2. Bataillon:	
Commander:	*Waffen-Hauptsturmführer* Maurice Berret
Aide:	Unknown
1. Kompanie Commander:	Unknown
2. Kompanie Commander:	*Waffen-Obesturmführer* Ivan Bartolomei
3. Kompanie Commander:	Unknown
4. Kompanie Commander:	*Waffen-Obersturmführer* Defever (*prawdopodobnie*)

Appendix IV

Gazetteer of Pomeranian Towns

Barkowo (Barkenfelde).
Barwice (Bärwalde).
Bezpraw (Kautzenberg).
Biały Bór (Baldenburg).
Biernatka (Bärenhütte).
Bińcze (Bärenwalde).
Bobolice (Bublitz).
Buczek (Butzke).
Buślary (Buslar).
Byszyno (Boissin).
Bytów (Bütow).
Chojnice (Konitz).
Chomętowo (Gumtow).
Choszczno (Arnswalde).
Ciechnowo (Technow).
Czaplin Mały (Klein Zaplin).
Czaplin Wielki (Gross Zaplin).
Czarne (Hammerstein).
Czarnowęsy (Zarnefanz).
Człuchów (Schlochau).
Dąbie (Altdamm).
Dębczyno (Denzin).
Drawno (Neuwedell).
Dygowo (Degow).
Dziwnów (Dievenow).
Goleniów (Gollnow).
Golce (Neugolz).
Górzyca (Görke).
Gruszewo (Grüssow).

Gryfice (Greifenberg in Pommern).
Jarzębniki (Falkenberg).
Jastrowie (Jastrow).
Karlino (Körlin).
Karnice (Karnitz).
Kamień Pomorski (Kammin).
Kamosowo (Kammisow).
Koczała (Flötenstein).
Kołczewo (Kolzow).
Koszalin (Köslin).
Kowańcz (Kawenz).
Krępsk (Krapsk).
Krzywopłoty (Stadtholzkathen).
Lubiatowo (Lindberg).
Lulewice (Alt Lülfitz).
Łazy (Laase).
Łeba (Leba).
Łeknica (Lucknitz).
Łęczno (Lenzen).
Łęczynko (Lenzen-Vorwek).
Łobez (Labes).
Łukęcin (Lüchtenthin).
Miastko (Rummelsburg).
Miechęcino (Mechentin).
Mierzyn (Alt Martin).
Międzyrzecze (Meseritz).
Międzywodzie (Heidebrink).
Międzyzdroje (Misdroy).
Miłocice (Falkenhagen).

Mirocice (Bullenwinkel).
Mrocza (Immenheim).
Mrzeżyno (Treptower Deep).
Nadarzyce (Rederitz).
Nadziejewo (Hansfelde).
Nakło (Nakel an der Netze).
Natolewice (Nebelfitz).
Niechorze (Ostseebad Horst).
Niekanin (Necknin).
Nosowo (Nassow).
Nowogard (Naugard).
Obroty (Wobrow).
Okonek (Ratzebuhr in Pommern).
Olszanów (Elsenau).
Osówko (Wutzow).
Ostre Bardo (Wusterbarth).
Ostropole (Osterfelde).
Piła (Schneidemühl).
Piotrowice (Peterfitz).
Płoty (Plathe).
Pniewo (Pinnow).
Pobłocie Wielkie (Groß Pobloth).
Pobierowo (Poberow).
Podgaje (Flederborn).
Polanów (Pollnow).
Police (Politz).
Połczyn Zdrój (Bad Polzin).
Pomianowo (Pumlow).
Poradz (Petersfelde).
Prosinko (Neudorf).
Przegonia (Heidekrug).
Przybiernowo (Pribbernow).
Pustkowo (Pustschow).
Pyrzyce (Pyritz).
Rąbino (Gross Rambin).
Recz (Reetz).
Redlino (Redlin).
Rogowo (Roggow).
Rościęcino (Rossenthin).
Rzecino (Retzin).
Rzeczenica (Stegers).
Rzyszczewo (Ristow).
Sępolno Wielkie (Gross Karzenburg).

Sławno (Schlawe).
Sławoborze (Stolzenberg).
Słosinko (Reinfeld).
Słowieńsko (Schlenzig).
Słupsk (Stolp).
Stanomino (Standemin).
Stargard (Stargard in Pommern).
Stary Borek (Altbork).
Stepnica (Stepenitz).
Stramnica (Alt Tramm}.
Suchań (Zachan).
Szczecin (Stetttin).
Szczecinek (Neustettin).
Szwecja (Freudenfier).
Świdwin (Schivelbein).
Świętouść (Swantuss).
Świnoujście (Swinemünde).
Trzebiatkowa (Radensfelde).
Trzebiatów (Treptow an der Rega).
Trzebiele (Komet).
Trzesieka (Streitzig).
Tychówko (Woldisch Tychow).
Ujście (Utz).
Uniechowo (Heinrichswalde).
Ustka (Stolpmünde).
Wałcz (Deutsch Krone).
Wapnica (Ravenstein).
Włodarka (Voigtshagen).
Zdbice (Stabitz).
Złotów (Flatow).
Żytelkowo (Siedkow).

Bibliography

Unpublished Archival Sources

Abschrift A 24/3. Heeresgruppe Weichsel. Anlagen zum Kriegstagebuch 21.1.45–31.1.45, United States National Archives, Microfilm T311 Roll 167.

Abschrift A 24/8. Befehl für die Verteidigung des Netze-Abschnittes Nr. 1. Heeresgruppe Weichsel. Anlagen zum Kriegstagebuch 21.1.45–31.1.45, United States National Archives, Microfilm T311 Roll 167.

Abschrift B 3/10. Fernspruch von Ingrid Alt 3.2. 17.45 Uhr, Heeresgruppe Weichsel. Anlagen zum Kriegstagebuch 1.2.45–14.2.45, United States National Archives, Microfilm T311 Roll 167.

Abschrift B 13/21. Heeresgruppe Weichsel. Anlagen zum Kriegstagebuch 1.2.45–14.2.45, United States National Archives, Microfilm T311 Roll 167.

Abschrift B 14/6. Heeresgruppe Weichsel. Anlagen zum Kriegstagebuch 1.2.45–14.2.45, United States National Archives, Microfilm T311 Roll 167.

Morgensmeldung vom 31.1.1945. Heeresgruppe Weichsel. Anlagen zum Kriegstagebuch 21.1.45–31.1.45, United States National Archives, Microfilm T311 Roll 167.

Morgensmeldung 10.2.45. Heeresgruppe Weichsel. Anlagen zum Kriegstagebuch 1.2.45–14.2.45, United States National Archives, Microfilm T311 Roll 167.

Morgensmeldung 11.2.45. Heeresgruppe Weichsel. Anlagen zum Kriegstagebuch 1.2.45–14.2.45, United States National Archives, Microfilm T311 Roll 167.

Morgensmeldung 14.2.45. Heeresgruppe Weichsel. Anlagen zum Kriegstagebuch 1.2.45–14.2.45, United States National Archives, Microfilm T311 Roll 167.

Morgensmeldung vom 17.2.45. Heeresgruppe Weichsel. Anlagen zum Kriegstagebuch 15.2.45–28.2.45, United States National Archives, Microfilm T311 Roll 168.

Tagebuch Nr 768/45. Heeresgruppe Weichsel. Anlagen zum Kriegstagebuch 21.1.45–31.1.45, United States National Archives, Microfilm T311 Roll 167.

Tagesmeldung vom 11.2.45. Heeresgruppe Weichsel. Anlagen zum Kriegstagebuch 1.2.45–14.2.45, United States National Archives, Microfilm T311 Roll 167, s. 2.

Tagesmeldung vom 21.2.45. Heeresgruppe Weichsel. Anlagen zum Kriegstagebuch 15.2.45–28.2.45, United States National Archives, Microfilm T311 Roll 168.

Listy oraz wspomnienia Waffen-Rottenführer Robert Soulat, podoficera kompanii sztabowej 33. Dywizji Grenadierów SS, rękopisy w zbiorach autora.

Relacja ogniomistrza Zenona Steina, żołnierza 8. Pułku Artylerii Haubic, nagranie zrealizowane w październiku 2010 r. w zbiorach autora.

Wspomnienia Alaine'a Boutiera, żołnierza 33. Dywizji Grenadierów SS, maszynopis w zbiorach autora.

Wspomnienia anonimowego żołnierza 33. Dywizji Grenadierów SS z archiwum Stanisława Kłoskowskiego z Olszanowa, kopie w zbiorach autora.

Wspomnienia Waffen-Untersturmführer Michel de Genouillac, maszynopis w zbiorach autora.

Published Archival Sources

Die Wehrmachtsberichte 1939–1945. Band 3: 1. Januar 1944 bis 9. Mai 1945. Orts-, Personen- und Formationsregister (Cologne: 1989).

Noce i dnie ... Ocalić od zapomnienia, praca zbiorowa zainicjowana przez Zespół Szkół im. Macieja Rataja w Gościnie, Gościno BDW.

Cisay, Michel, 'Francuski esesman', *Kwartalnik Historyczny Ośrodka Karta*, Nr 48 (Warsaw: 2006).

De La Mazière, Christian, *Marzyciel w hełmie. Francuz w Waffen SS* (Warsaw: 2005).

Degrelle, Léon, *Front wschodni 1941–1945* (Krakow: 2007).

Degrelle, Léon, *The History of the Waffen-SS, zapis przemówienia wygłoszonego na forum Asociación cultural* 'Amigos de Léon Degrelle', Madryt BDW.

Himmler, Heinrich, *Die Schutzstaffeln als antibolschewistische Kampforganisation* (Munich: 1937).

Kienitz, Werner, *Der Wehrkreis II vor dem Zusammenbruch des Reiches* (Hamburg: 1955).

Lindenblatt, Helmut, *Pommern 1945: Eines der letzten Kapitel in der Geschichte vom Untergant des Dritten Reiches* (Würzburg: 2008).

Sroga, Alojzy, *Na drodze stał Kołobrzeg* (Warsaw: 1980).

Steiner, Felix, *Ochotnicy Waffen-SS. Idea i poświęcenie* (Gdańsk: 2010).

Verton, Hendrik, *W piekle frontu wschodniego. Byłem holenderskim ochotnikiem w Waffen-SS* (Warsaw: 2010).

Books

33. Waffen-Grenadier-Division der SS Charlemagne 1944–1945, artykuł opublikowany w ramach witryny internetowej dedivisioncharlemagne.net przez autora posługującego się pseudonimem Vincent.

Wspomnienia Otto Holznagla z Białogardu opublikowane w ramach projektu *Altes Land Belgard*, tłum. Łukasz Gładysiak.

Baxter, Ian, *Ostatnie lata Waffen-SS* (Warsaw: 2010).

Bishop, Christopher, *SS: Hell on the Western Front* (St Paul: 2003).

Blandford, Edmund, *Hitler's Second Army. The Waffen-SS* (Shrewsbury: 1994).

Brzeziński, Piotr, *Ocena szans operacji zaczepnej o kryptonimie 'Sonnenwende' na podstawie analizy możliwości niemieckich wojsk pancernych w końcowym etapie*

II wojny światowej. Luty 1945 <pomorze1945.com/file.php?file=17> (accessed 22.08.2012 r.).

Duffy, Christopher, *Red Storm on the Reich: The Soviet March on Germany 1945* (London: 1991).

Forbes, Robert, *For Europe. The French Volunteers of the Waffen-SS* (Solihull: 2006).

Gładysiak, Łukasz, 'Batalion Alarmowy Hempel', *Głos Kołobrzegu*, Friday 28 February 2014 (Koszalin: 2014).

Gładysiak, Łukasz, 'Belgard w rękach Sowietów', *Głos Koszalina*, Friday 6 March 2015 (Koszalin: 2015).

Gładysiak, Łukasz, 'Francuscy SS-mani w Karścinie', *Głos ma Historia*, 25 November 2013 (Koszalin: 2013).

Gładysiak, Łukasz, 'Generał von Tettau w Białogardzie', *Głos Koszalina*, Friday 15 May 2015 (Koszalin: 2015).

Gładysiak, Łukasz, 'Krucjata antybolszewicka', *II wojna światowa. Wydarzenia – ludzie – bojowe szlaki*, Vol. IV.

Gładysiak, Łukasz, 'Lwia głowa' w Białogardzie, *Głos Koszalina*, Friday 9 January 2015 (Koszalin: 2015).

Gładysiak, Łukasz, 'Przełamanie Wału Pomorskiego. Działania 1. Armii Wojska Polskiego od 30 stycznia do 11 lutego 1945 r.', *Militaria XX wieku. Wydanie Specjalne*, nr 1 (17) (Lublin: 2011).

Hale, Christopher, *Hitler's Foreign Executioners. Europe's Dirty Secret* (Stroud: 2011).

Klasik, Marian, *Dziwnowski Front. Walki o przesmyk Dziwnowski*, <http://koszalin7.pl/st/pom/pomorze_302.html> (accessed 2.09.2012 r.).

Klasik, Marian, *Ziemia Kamieńska przed 65 laty* <http://www.uzdrowisko.kamienpomorski.pl/news.php?readmore=1076> (accessed 31.08.2012 r.).

Kroczyński, Hieronim, *Kronika Kołobrzegu* (Kołobrzeg: 2000).

Lambert, Pierre-Philippe and Le Marec, Gérard, *Les Français sous le casque allemand* (Paris: 2002).

Landwehr, Richard, *French Volunteers of the Waffen-SS* (Bennington: 2006).

Lefèvre, Eric, '*Charlemagne* meurt sur l'Oder. Les combats de la division française des Waffen-SS en Poméranie Orientale: Février–Mars 1945', *Batailles. Histoire Militaire du XXe Siècle*, nr 6 (Paris: 2005).

Lindenblatt, Helmut, *Pommern 1945. Eines der letzten Kapitel in der Geschichte vom Untergant des Dritten Reiches* (Würzburg: 2008).

Littlejohn ,David, *Foreign Legions of the Third Reich. Vol. 1: Norway, Denmark, France* (San Jose: 1979).

Littlejohn, David, *Political Traitors* (London: 1972).

Mabire, Jean, *Mourir á Berlin* (Paris: 1997).

Miniewicz, Janusz, and Bogusław, Perzyk, *Wał Pomorski* (Warsaw: 1997).

Musiał, Ludwik, *Pod skrzydłami Anioła. Kościół Św. Michała Archanioła w Karlinie ma 500 lat* (Karlino: 2010).

Partacz, Czesław, 'Wyzwolenie Białogardu' in *Białogard 1299–1999. Studia z dziejów miasta* (Białogard: 1999).

Pigoreau, Olivier, 'Rendez-vous tragique à Mengen', *Batailles. Histoire Militaire du XXe Siècle*, nr 34 (Paris: 2009).

Ramme, Alwin, *Służba Bezpieczeństwa SS* (Warsaw: 1984).

Ripley, Tim, *Hitler's Praetorians: The History of the Waffen-SS 1925–1945* (Staplehurst: 2004).

Roszkowski, Jakub, 'Mogiła niemieckich żołnierzy w Białogardzie wciąż ukryta', Głos Koszaliński, 12 October 2011 r.

Saint-Loup, Louis, *Les hérétiques* (Paris: 1965).

Szarota, Tomasz, *U progu zagłady. Zajścia antyżydowskie i pogromy w okupowanej Europie – Warszawa, Paryż, Amsterdam, Antwerpia, Kowno* (Warsaw: 2000).

Szopa, Maciej, 'Przestrzeń dla rasy panów', *II wojna światowa. Wydarzenia – ludzie – bojowe szlaki*, Vol IV.

Tieke, Wilhlem, *Tragödie um die Treue. Kampf und Untergang des III (germ.) SS-Panzer-Korps* (Osnabrück: 1978).

Trigg, Jonathan, *Hitler's Gauls: The History of the 33rd Waffen-SS Division Charlemagne* (Staplehurst: 2006).

Williamson, Gordon, *The SS: Hitler's Instrument of Terror* (London: 1995).

Index